Abraham

MEN *of*
CHARACTER

Abraham

Holding Fast to the Will of God

GENE A. GETZ

Foreword by O.S. Hawkins

B&H
PUBLISHING GROUP

Nashville, Tennessee

Published by:
Broadman & Holman, Publishers
Nashville, Tennessee

ISBN: 9780805461671

Dewey Decimal Classification: 248.842
Subject Heading: Abraham \ Christian Life \ Men—Religious Life
Library of Congress Card Catalog Number: 95–43168

Unless otherwise noted, Scripture quotations are from the Holy Bible, New International Version, copyright © 1973, 1978, 1984 by International Bible Society; other versions used are the New American Standard Bible (NASB), © the Lockman Foundation, 1960, 1962, 1963, 1968, 1971, 1972, 1973, 1975, 1977; used by permission; and the King James Version (KJV).

Library of Congress Cataloging-in-Publication Data
Getz, Gene A.
    [When you're cofused & uncertain]
    Abraham : holding fast to the will of God / Gene A. Getz.
        p. cm. — (Men of character)
    Originally published : When you're confused & uncertain
    Includes bibliographical references.
    ISBN 0-8054-6167-1 (TP)
    1. Abraham. (Biblical patriarch) 2. Patriarchs (Bible)—Biography.
3. Bible. O.T.—Biography. I. Title. II. Series: Getz, Gene A. Men of character.
BS580.A3G43   1996
95-43168
CIP

10 11 12 13 14 15   10 09 08 07

*T*his book on Abraham is sincerely dedicated to my good friend and fellow minister of the gospel, O. S. Hawkins. O.S. serves as senior pastor at the historic First Baptist Church in downtown Dallas, Texas. He has risen to the distinct challenge in becoming the third pastor of this great church, following in the giant footsteps of George W. Truett and W. A. Criswell, who respectively served this congregation for more than fifty years. I personally consider O.S. one of the unique men of character who is serving Jesus Christ faithfully as we march toward the twenty-first century. It's a privilege to serve God together in the great and needy area identified as the Dallas Metroplex.

Contents

Foreword

*O*ne of my great personal joys in moving to the city of Dallas has been getting to know the Christ alive in Gene Getz. Like thousands of others in the Western world, I have known him for years through the printed pages of his books. To be the recipient of his personal encouragement is a blessing beyond my ability to describe.

Gene and I first met at a large outdoor rally centered around a moral issue in our city of Dallas. The two of us were the only pastors in the midst of a few hundred laypersons. We needed each other that day, and our hearts were knitted together. I have watched him practice in the normal traffic patterns of which he writes and speaks. He stands strong and tall on moral issues but is always seasoned with grace and restoration.

The present massive men's movement is a modern phenomenon. But it did not just happen. It is the product of years of cultivation and nurture. One of God's greatest tools in softening the soil of hundreds of thousands of men's hearts has been Gene's best-selling volume, *The Measure of a Man.* We use the word *classic* with far too much regularity in our day, but this book is a men's classic in the truest sense of the word and a must-read for anyone serious about becoming a godly man.

Now from his prolific pen comes the next volume in his series on men of character. In this series we have learned from David's life to seek God faithfully, from Elijah to remain steadfast through days of uncertainty, from Nehemiah to become a disciplined leader, and from Joshua to be a consistent role model. In the volume you hold in your hand, Gene brings

Father Abraham out of the pages of Scripture into our own contemporary culture to show each of us the importance of holding fast to the will of God. Happy and productive is the man who not only reads these pages but heeds them and applies them to his daily life.

O. S. Hawkins
First Baptist Church
Dallas, Texas

Introduction

Think for a moment about what is happening in American culture. To help you gain a realistic perspective, open your newspaper, look at the entertainment section, and read the subjects that are being discussed on television talk shows—commonly referred to as "Trash TV." It is not uncommon to see such topics as husbands who cheat, adulterous wives, unfaithful lovers, transvestism, sex changes, homosexual lovers, group sex, and a myriad of subtopics that deal with these issues in more specific and explicit ways.

"But that's not the norm," you say. Perhaps. But when I see what's happening, I can't help but reflect on what Paul described in his letter to the Romans. In chapter 1 we see God giving people over to sexual impurity (heterosexual sins, 1:24), shameful lusts (homosexual sins, 1:26), and depraved minds (every kind of wickedness, 1:28–29), a perfect description of the lifestyles paraded on "Trash TV."

In chapter 2, however, Paul directed his barbs to those who claim to be religious and yet do the same thing, perhaps behind closed doors. Studies reveal that a lot of sinful behavior is not that visible. And what about those of us who would never do those things, we say, yet we participate by watching and being entertained. Many of us, even as Christians, are talking out of both sides of our mouths.

A Universal Picture

Interestingly, what Paul described in the early chapters of the Book of Romans is a universal picture of humanity that cycles through history, much the same way John described the state of Christianity when he recorded Jesus' messages to the seven churches in the Book of Revelation (Rev. 2:1–3:22). Jesus was speaking to churches that existed in the first century in the province of Asia, but what He described is also a universal picture of various kinds of churches throughout history. What Paul wrote in Romans 1 and 2 also describes the world of his day. But under the divine guidance of the Holy Spirit, this scenario describes the world at various periods in history, certainly going back to the days when a man named Abraham worshiped idols in Ur of the Chaldeans.

In His sovereign grace, God chose Abraham and his family to be the means to bring the message of redemption to a world of people who had deteriorated to the point that they did not even "think it worthwhile to retain the knowledge of God" (Rom. 1:28). Abram, later called Abraham, responded to God's call and became the father of us all in terms of finding our way back to God.

Back to Our Roots

Welcome to an exciting study of a man's life that takes us back to the very roots of Christianity. Next to Jesus Christ, Abraham is one of the most significant men mentioned in the Bible. Moses, of course, stands out as the greatest prophet and leader in Israel (Deut. 34:10).[1] But if it were not for Abraham, there would have been no nation to lead. In fact, if God had not chosen Abraham out of the degenerate and pagan community in which he lived, there may have been no savior of the world, for it was from Abraham's seed that Jesus Christ came to bless all nations. The study of Abraham's life then is indeed a study of God's great redemptive plan. I trust you'll read carefully and prayerfully, asking God to help you become God's man in today's world just as Abraham became God's man in his day.

Chapter 1

God's Great Redemptive Plan
Read 1 Genesis 12:1–3

*A*merican culture is reeling from the impact of deviant sexual behavior. The AIDS epidemic is at an all-time high and threatens to become even more destructive. However, the current great moral debate in American culture focuses on two major issues: music videos and hard-core pornography on the Internet. Rap music features violence against women and openly, unashamedly describes sex in terms that affront average human beings. Additionally, the great Internet "explosion" features sexual explicitness that brings every form of deviation into the home and can be accessed easily by children. A recent report indicated that the more violent and deviant sex may be portrayed, including bestiality, the greater the demand for it. Some have estimated that 85 percent of the graphics that are swapped and downloaded are pornographic.

A Familiar Story

What's happening in our high-tech society is far removed in many respects from the culture of Abraham's day. But one thing remains the same: we "all have sinned and fall short of the glory of God" (Rom. 3:23). Furthermore, we all have a natural tendency to deteriorate morally and ethically and to chose to follow our sinful ways. Our technology only helps to speed up and multiply the process worldwide. But, in essence, mankind has been the same ever since Adam and Eve introduced sin into the world. This is why God put into motion His great redemptive plan by calling Abraham out of his own sinful environment to be a blessing to "all peoples on the earth" (Gen. 12:3).

A Friend of God

Abraham's place in God's redemptive plan is evident from the titles used to describe him, the amount of space used to record the events of his life, and the way he is mentioned in the New Testament. He is identified as the friend of God (2 Chron. 20:7; Isa. 41:8; James 2:23), and the authors of Scripture often refer to the "God of Abraham." More than twelve chapters in the Book of Genesis are devoted to describing Abraham's life, and in the New Testament Abraham is referred to in four prominent letters: Romans, Galatians, Hebrews, and James. In most of these first-century references, the biblical writers used Abraham's life to illustrate how we can be saved—the great theme of Scripture.

Beginning at the Beginning

The story of Abraham begins in Genesis 12, which in many respects is where the main story of the Bible begins. What precedes in the opening chapters of Genesis represents compressed history. The Holy Spirit tells us about the creation of the universe, including Adam and Eve. But we also see the origin of sin, which resulted from the way in which Adam and Eve disobeyed God. We're also exposed to the first murder, when Cain killed his brother Abel (Genesis 4).

From that point forward, we see the rapid multiplication and spread of violence and wickedness, which culminated in the flood that was God's judgment on a sin-sick society. But because "Noah was a righteous man, blameless among the people of his time" and because "he walked with God," Noah "found favor in the eyes of the Lord" and was preserved along with his family (Gen. 6:8–9).

After the flood, men and women again multiplied on the earth. But as we might predict, God's highest creation soon turned away from Him. The deterioration was even greater than before the flood.

Spiraling Downward

Note the way in which men and women followed a downward path of sin. First, they "exchanged the glory of the immortal God for images made to look like mortal man." Then they began to worship "birds and animals and reptiles" (Rom. 1:23).

When my wife and I visited the city of Rome several years ago, I was captivated by the statuary of the Roman emperors. It is no secret, of course, that these men set themselves up as gods to be worshiped and venerated. What is left of these Roman ruins is a testimony to the judgment they brought on themselves. The amazing Roman Colosseum still stands, but only as a shell of what it once was when the blood of men and animals flowed freely as the spectators screamed for more. This kind of brutal entertainment also became their "gods."

Sexual Impurity

The first step downward involved sexual immorality among men and women. The sacred act of love between a husband and wife gave way to premarital and extramarital sex, open marriages, prostitution, and group sex. Paul's words are descriptive and explicit: "Therefore God gave them over in the sinful desires of their hearts to *sexual impurity* for the degrading of their bodies with one another. They exchanged the truth of God for a lie, and worshiped and served created things rather than the Creator—who is forever praised" (Rom. 1:24–25).[1]

Sex also became their god. They were obsessed by it, controlled by it, and sold their souls to their passions and uncontrolled lusts, which led to the next step downward.

Shameful Lusts

At this point, Paul became even more explicit. He described this kind of behavior, not just as sexual impurity, but as shameful lusts: "Because of this, God gave them over to *shameful lusts.* Even their women exchanged natural relations for unnatural ones. In the same way the men also abandoned natural relations with women and were inflamed with lust for one another. Men committed indecent acts with other men, and received in themselves the due penalty for their perversion" (Rom. 1:26–27).

In society at large, men initially lead the way in creating an immoral environment. Before long, women follow and they soon gain control because of the power associated with female sexuality. It becomes a powerful weapon they can use for self-protection and what women perceive as fulfillment.

In view of human sexuality in general, this is startling. Paul underscored this point when he stated that *"even* their women exchanged natural relations for unnatural ones" (1:26). In other words, Paul seems to be saying that it's not as surprising when this happens to men, but when women resort to this sinful practice, we've reached a new low point in our degradation.

Every Kind of Wickedness

Sexual immorality leads the way in moving away from God's plan for our lives. The final step involves evil practices of all kinds that become a part of this toboggan slide of sin that impacts total humanity. Again, listen to Paul's report:

> Furthermore, since they did not think it worthwhile to retain the knowledge of God, he gave them over to a *depraved mind,* to do what ought not to be done. They have become filled with *every kind of wickedness, evil, greed and depravity.* They are full of envy, murder, strife, deceit and malice. They are gossips, slanderers, God-haters, insolent, arrogant and boastful; they invent ways of doing evil; they disobey their parents; they are senseless, faithless, heartless, ruthless. Although they know God's righteous

decree that those who do such things deserve death, they not only continue to do these very things but also approve of those who practice them. (Rom. 1:28–32)

Back to Square One

What a tragedy. When God purified and cleansed the earth from sin by means of the flood, He gave men and women another chance to walk with Him. Eventually, all human beings turned away from God and went their own sinful ways. But God is also a God of love. Even though His wrath was being revealed through the natural consequences of sin, He once again extended His loving hand and gave all of us another chance.

Don't misunderstand. God hates our sin, but He still loves us. So, in the midst of this human decadence that once again permeated the earth following the flood, God began to unveil a marvelous and final plan to provide redemption for all mankind. It began with one man, Abraham, through whom He promised to bless all nations in spite of their resentment and hostility toward Him.

The Lord Had Said to Abram . . .

When God first spoke to Abraham (Gen. 12:1a), Abraham's name was Abram,[2] which means "exalted father." Years later, God changed his name to Abraham, which means "father of a multitude" (17:5).

A Sovereign Choice

When God chose Abraham out of a pagan and sinful culture, it was a sovereign choice. We're not told why, out of other possible candidates, God decided to choose Abraham. But we do know from Noah's example (6:8–9) that when God deals with us, He begins His acts of mercy by communicating with those whose hearts are open to truth. From his response to

God's call, Abraham seemed to be this kind of man, although he was just as steeped in idolatry as his father (Josh. 24:2).

We must understand that no matter what Abraham's attitude or lifestyle, God's decision to choose him was purely a sovereign choice. Abraham became the "father of us all" because of God's grace and mercy (Rom. 4:16). Furthermore, it was because of his response to God's call that he eventually became righteous in God's sight. Again, listen to Paul's words in Romans. After demonstrating that "all have sinned and fall short of the glory of God," including both Jews and Gentiles, Paul declared that Abraham was also "justified through faith" (Rom. 5:1). More specifically, Paul wrote:

> What then shall we say that Abraham, our forefather, discovered in this matter? If, in fact, Abraham was justified by works, he had something to boast about—but not before God. What does the Scripture say? "Abraham believed God, and it was credited to him as righteousness." (Rom. 4:1–3)

Isn't This Favoritism?

Some people are troubled by the fact that when God unveiled His salvation plan, He began by choosing Abraham. They accuse God of playing favorites. However, those who think this way don't understand that all human beings were lost at this time and by choice. Again, as Paul stated in his letter to the Romans: "There is no one righteous, not even one; there is no one who understands, no one who seeks for God. All have turned away, they have together become worthless; there is no one who does good, not even one" (Rom. 3:10–12).

This statement applies to all men and women to one degree or another in all periods of history. But it was particularly true when God reached out to Abraham. God's particularism in this instance was a means to make salvation a universal possibility for all of us. This was an act of God's mercy, an act of reaching out to sinful humanity. Through Abraham, God unfolded a plan to make salvation available to the whole world.

Why Not Choose Another Method?

Although God is all-powerful, it would be contrary to His holy nature to suddenly pardon sinful humanity. He simply cannot do that. Rather, He chose a process leading to the one final and great sacrifice—the sacrifice of His own Son (Heb. 1:1–2; 10:1–10). Furthermore, He also chose a method that would—because of His patience, longsuffering, and grace—take time to get His message to all people in the world. If we are Christians, we are responsible to implement this great plan, to make sure this message of hope is proclaimed to all nations (Matt. 28:19–20).

God's Time Clock

One thing is very clear regarding the penalty for sin. God does not act without warnings. Before He destroyed the world with the flood, He had Noah spend 120 years building an ark and preaching that judgment was coming (1 Pet. 3:20; 2 Pet. 2:5).

The second time around, God decided to extend His grace even further, a plan that would last not just 120 years, but, to date, nearly 4,000 years. Step by step, He is unfolding this plan, using a variety of approaches to try to get our attention regarding the judgment that is coming. The plan is outlined succinctly in Genesis 12:1–3. As we've seen, it began with God's choice of Abraham.

A Sin-sick Society

Nearly four thousand years ago, Abraham lived in an ancient city called Ur, one of the most important cities in the world. It was a busy commercial center in the country of Mesopotamia, on the Persian Gulf and bordered by the Euphrates River. Ur covered about four square miles and had a population of nearly three hundred thousand people. Many were proficient in mathematics, advanced in astronomy, and specialized in weaving and engraving. They even preserved their knowledge by writing on clay tablets, which has been invaluable to archae-ologists in reconstructing the social and religious life of these people.

We've already noted the depravity that existed, if indeed Paul was describing the world at this time. These people worshiped many gods, particularly nature gods. In the center of Ur was a large temple, called a ziggurat, where the people worshiped their chief deity, a moon god called Nanna.

A Sudden Appearance

Abraham probably lived with his family on the outskirts of Ur. His father, Terah, was a shepherd who had settled in the rich pasturelands surrounding the city. Predictably, the religious influence of the culture had penetrated this family. They too—including Abraham and his wife Sarah—worshiped idols.

It was in the midst of this idolatrous and affluent environ-ment that God suddenly appeared to Abraham, commanded him to break his family ties, to leave the city of Ur, and to head off for a place he'd never been before. More specifically, God said, "Leave your country, your people and your father's household and go to the land I will show you" (Gen. 12:1).

What a shock this must have been to Abraham. As far as we know, he had never experienced anything like this before. Was this real or a figment of his imagination? Questions must have flooded his mind. Before he could reflect too much on this unusual experience, God gave him more information, promises that must have boggled his mind.

Three Promises

God promised Abraham three things: a land, a large family that would become a great nation, and a special blessing that would affect everyone on the earth (Gen. 12:1–3). More specifically, God said: "Go to the *land* I will show you. I will make you into a *great nation* and I will bless you; I will make your name great, and you will be a *blessing*. I will *bless* those who *bless* you, and whoever curses you I will curse; and all peoples on earth will be *blessed* through you" (Gen. 12:1b-3).

The land was Canaan, a place Abraham didn't even know existed. The "great nation" referred to Israel, something Abraham could not comprehend at this moment. And the "blessing" referred to the birth of Jesus Christ, a great truth that would affect his own eternal destiny, the destiny of his immediate family, and eventually all the people who would comprise the nation of Israel. This blessing would then impact millions of people on the earth for centuries to come, including you and me.

Dr. George Peters spoke to this point when he wrote, "Israel's history is not a history of arbitrary election, of favoritism, of narrow particularism and nationalism. It is an act of sovereign and gracious election to preserve the race and the temporal and eternal destiny of mankind."[3]

Becoming God's Man Today

Principles to Live By

Principle 1. God is a merciful and loving God who is reaching out to all humanity.

God still wants us to know His will. When the whole world was lost and in a state of active rebellion against God, He sovereignly chose one man who would be an initial part of a redemptive plan that would affect the world in centuries to come.

God's redemptive plan is still unfolding. Although the descendants of Abraham failed God many times and turned from His divine purpose, God's mercy continues. His promises to Abraham cannot be broken. They are unconditional. Because of God's grace, the world has continued for nearly four thousand years. God's message of salvation has been heralded continually, at times weak and almost inaudible, but it has never been silenced.

Before Jesus Christ invaded planet Earth, God spoke to the world primarily through the nation Israel. Since the first century, He has been speaking to the world through the church, the body of Christ. This is why Jesus prayed in the presence of His disciples: "My prayer is not for them alone. I pray also for those who will believe in me through their message, that all of them may be one, Father, just as you are in me and I am in you. May they also be in us *so that the world may believe that you have sent me. . . . May they be brought to complete unity to let the world know that you sent me and have loved them even as you have loved me"* (John 17:20–21, 23).

Principle 2. God is long-suffering toward lost humanity, patiently waiting for men and women to respond to His love and grace.

Throughout history, people have misunderstood God's long-suffering and patience. This was true in the days of Noah. They did not understand that "God waited patiently . . . while the ark was being built" (1 Pet. 3:20). Following the death and resurrection of Jesus Christ, people also very quickly lost sight of this truth. Just so today people do not understand God's patience in withholding judgment on the earth. Listen to the apostle Peter in his second letter:

> First of all, you must understand that in the last days *scoffers will come,* scoffing and following their own evil desires. They will say, *"Where is this 'coming' he promised?* Ever since our fathers died, everything goes on as it has since the beginning of creation." . . . But do not forget this one thing, dear friends: *With the Lord a day is like a thousand years, and a thousand years are like a day.* The Lord is not slow in keeping his promise, as some understand slowness. *He is patient with you, not wanting anyone to perish, but everyone to come to repentance.* (2 Pet. 3:3–4, 8–9)

Today we look back to the life, death, and resurrection of Jesus Christ, the One who would make available a blessing for all families of the earth. We are among those who "are blessed along with Abraham, the man of faith" (Gal. 3:9). We are participants in God's marvelous grace, for if God had not reached down that day and called Abraham, the world would have continued on a collision course that would have led to total destruction and annihilation, followed by eternal judgment and separation from God.

Personalizing These Principles

Do You Know Christ Personally?

What is your personal relationship with Jesus Christ? Are you ready to meet Him should you die or should He suddenly appear the second time? Don't reject His love, His patience, His grace.

Someday He will come, and if you have not accepted His plan for your life it will be too late. The door of salvation, like the door of the ark, will be closed. God will then turn His face away from those who have rejected Him. The Bible says, "It is a dreadful thing to fall into the hands of the living God" (Heb. 10:31).

Receive Jesus Christ Today

God's grace at this moment is still available. Accept His gift of salvation. This prayer will help you. Pray it meaningfully by writing your name in the blanks provided.

Father, I thank you for sending the Lord Jesus Christ to be my personal Savior from sin. And I, _____, confess that I am a sinner, that I have fallen short of your perfect standard. And I thank you that just as you called Abraham out of a pagan world, you are also calling me. And I, _____, now receive the Lord Jesus Christ as my Savior from sin. I believe He died for me personally. I, at this moment, repent and turn from my own way to following Jesus Christ who is the way, the truth, and the life. Thank you for coming into my life and making me a Christian.

Set a Goal

As you reflect on these two dynamic principles, ask yourself two questions:

1. Have I received the gospel of the Lord Jesus Christ by believing that He died and rose again for me?

2. If I have received the gospel and know Christ personally, am I sharing this wonderful message of salvation with others who do not understand God's good news?

Based on the answers to these questions, write out a personal goal:

_____

_____

_____

_____

Memorize the Following Scripture

Commit the following Scripture to memory in order to help you realize your goal:

> *Therefore, since we have been justified through faith, we have peace with God through our Lord Jesus Christ, through whom we have gained access by faith into this grace in which we now stand. And we rejoice in the hope of the glory of God.*
> ROMANS 5:1–2

Growing Together

The following questions are designed for small-group discussion. Read together Hebrews 11:8–12. Use this passage as a springboard to review this chapter on God's great redemptive plan.

1. Can you remember a particular time in your life when you heard God speak through the Scriptures regarding your need to accept the Lord Jesus Christ as your personal savior? Would you share with the group what happened?

2. Let's role-play for a moment. Who will volunteer to share the message of the gospel with a member of our group who asks the following question: What must I do to be saved?

3. How would you respond to someone who states that God showed favoritism when He chose Abraham and the nation of Israel to be His special people?

4. What can we pray for you particularly?

Chapter 2

Following God Fully
Read Genesis 12:1–9

I remember receiving a telephone call one day from a fellow professor. The year was 1968. The man on the other end of the line was Dr. Howard Hendricks. At that time, I was a member of the faculty at Moody Bible Institute. He was a professor at Dallas Theological Seminary.

"Gene," he said, "I want to invite you to come to Dallas to be my associate in the Christian Education Department."

Needless to say, I was rather startled. This call was a total surprise.

"I'm going on sabbatical for a year," he continued, "and I need someone to take my place. When I return, we'll team the ministry together."

Although deeply honored with this invitation, I was very hesitant to allow myself to take this opportunity too seriously. After all, I had "cut my teeth" at Moody. It felt like family. I was part of the brick and mortar having just completed the writing of the official history of Moody Bible Institute. Furthermore, I wasn't sure I wanted to make the jump from teaching undergraduate studies to interacting with graduate students.

However, the more my wife and I prayed about this new challenge, the more convinced we became that we needed to at least visit Dallas and explore the possibility of making this move. After a few days' investigating, asking questions, and visiting classes, we knew what we should do. We decided to move to Dallas.

Was this a difficult move? Not really. It happens all the time in our society. This kind of decision, of course, always presents some unique challenges: leaving friends, family, and brothers and sisters in Christ we had come to love. Then there's the challenge of developing new relationships. But we *knew* where we were going. We'd been there. We'd even arranged to build a new home that was waiting for us when we arrived. We immediately found a new church and were welcomed warmly into the fellowship.

Contrasts and Similarities

What a contrast with Abraham's call. He didn't even know where he was going. He'd never been to Canaan. He didn't have a map, let alone access to a moving company that could transport his personal belongings to wherever it was God was leading him.

Nevertheless, what happened to Abraham in the journey he was about to begin is uniquely related to all of us. Although he faced challenges we'll never face, the dynamics of knowing and following God's will are virtually the same for Christians of all time. From Abraham's life flow powerful principles to live by.

The Lord's message to Abraham must have been very clear and convincing. No man in his right mind would leave his country, his relatives, and his immediate family to head off for an unknown destination without being utterly convinced it was the right thing to do. But the insecurity associated with this move must have been frightening. Think of the challenge he faced just to convince his wife, Sarah, that this was an intelligent decision.

For nearly sixty years Abraham had lived in a community of people who bowed to the gods of nature. Idolatry permeated his family life. He had never heard of the God who had saved Noah and his family from a watery grave. But suddenly and unexpectedly, this God appeared to Abraham. What an awesome moment it must have been. Initially, he must have been astonished and skeptical.

We're not told how all this transpired. But one thing seems certain: God did not leave much room for Abraham to question the reality of this experience. God not only spoke (Gen. 12:1), but the New Testament indicates that Abraham actually saw God (Acts 7:2).

Struggles and Tensions

Understandably, when Abraham made this decision to obey God, he faced some very real difficulties and inward struggles (Gen. 11:31; Acts 7:2–4). God told him to make a complete break with his idolatrous environment, even leaving behind his parents and his relatives. This was a serious decision, involving not only relational tension but economic repercussions.

Let's imagine what may have happened. Based upon what we know from the biblical text, the conversation could have gone like this:

ABRAM: Dad, you're not going to believe what happened to me!

TERAH: Oh, really, son. Tell me about it.

ABRAM: Well . . . I know there is a God greater than all gods! I have seen Him! He talked with me!

TERAH: Abram, I told you to stay out of the wine cellar. Right?

ABRAM: Yes, dad. But I haven't been drinking. It's true. I've seen Him and I've heard Him.

TERAH: You're really serious aren't you? You say you've seen Him and heard Him?

ABRAM: Yes, dad. I saw Him in a glorious manifestation. I couldn't see His face, but I could make out an outline of His person. And I heard His voice clearly, just as clearly as I'm hearing yours right now.

TERAH: Well, what in the world did He say?

ABRAM: Well, it may sound strange, but He told me to pack up and leave Ur.

TERAH: To what?

ABRAM: To leave Ur and the whole land and . . .

TERAH: And what, Abram?

ABRAM: To . . . to leave you behind, dad. To leave my brothers, my cousins—to leave all my relatives.

TERAH: Nonsense! You *have* been drinking!

ABRAM: No, dad, it's true. And it's real. It was no dream. I've got to follow this call. I must obey, even though I don't know where this place is and I don't know much about this God. But I'm convinced He has more power than all of our gods here in Mesopotamia.

TERAH: But you can't just start out without knowing where you're headed!

ABRAM: But God said He'd show me a new land, and I believe Him.

TERAH: Abram, you've been hallucinating. This is absolute nonsense. You're sick. You must have a fever.

ABRAM: I'm not ill, Dad. And I'm not drunk.

TERAH: This is crazy! Didn't this God give you any clue as to where in the world He wanted you to go?

ABRAM: Well, He mentioned a land called Canaan, somewhere in the west. And what's more, God promised that He would make me a great nation and eventually—through me—all the families of the earth would be blessed.

TERAH: Son, you're not going alone. This God you speak of must have something very special for you, and I'm not going to miss it. I have always wanted to be something other than a shepherd. I'm going with you. And we're taking Lot with us, too. You'll remember, I promised my brother before he died that I would take good care of his son. So let's start packing.

Although the biblical text doesn't give us many details, God's appearance to Abraham had to have led to some intense interaction between him and his father. In fact, Terah somehow got in the driver's seat, and they started out *together*, under his father's leadership. Abraham didn't make a complete break with Terah as God had told him to. Allowing this to happen, Abraham's obedience was only partial.

On the Way

Even though Abraham did not obey God completely, he began the trip from Ur to Haran. He took Sarah, his wife, and together with his father and his nephew, Lot, they began the long trip along the Euphrates River (see fig. 1). There is also some biblical evidence that Terah's brother, Nahor, and his family may have also joined with them, although it is possible that they moved to Haran later (Gen. 11:29; 22:20–23; 24:10; 27:43).

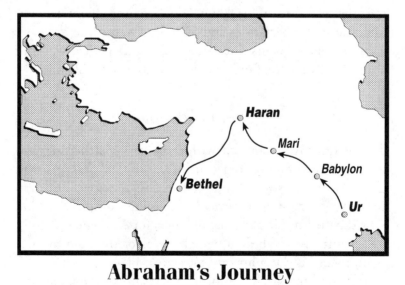

Abraham's Journey

Fig. 1

A Fifteen-Year Delay

When Abraham and his family arrived in Haran, a city just as idolatrous as Ur and still in the land of Mesopotamia, we read that they "settled there" (11:31). This too was a step out of God's perfect will. Scholars calculate Abraham resided in Haran approximately fifteen years before he finally journeyed on to the land of promise. As we'll see, this additional disobedience eventually caused Abraham a great deal of stress, pain, and outward trouble.

God's Patience

I believe we're also seeing God's patience. Although the Lord wanted Abraham to make a decisive break with his family, He also understood how difficult this would be, particularly considering the cultural and emotional ties that existed in this kind of extended family. Although "family life" according to God's plan had deteriorated greatly in this culture, Abraham's family was still intact and strongly bonded. Terah was the head of this ancient household, and he commanded respect from the other members of his family. Abraham was caught between these cultural expectations and what God wanted. In this case, cultural commitments interfered with God's perfect will, but at the same time the Lord understood Abraham's dilemma.

On to Canaan

The security Abraham felt within his family structure temporarily caused him to forget the details of God's call. As with all of us, the passing of time blurred his memory. But even though Abraham had difficulty obeying completely, God waited patiently. He had a definite plan for Abraham (12:4–5).

Eventually Terah died, which enabled Abraham to once again focus his thoughts on God's great plan and will for his life. We read that he "went forth *as the Lord had spoken to him;*

and Lot went with him." At this point in time, "Abram was seventy-five years old" (Gen. 12:4, NASB).[1]

An Easy First Step

Traveling from Ur to Haran was a rather secure move in some respects, like my own move from Illinois to Texas. Abraham had maintained his close family ties, and they were heading for a familiar city. Culturally, religiously, and in most every way there was little change in their environment.

Remember too that the trip from Ur to Haran was not overly difficult. In some ways it was like taking a superhighway rather than a gravel road. They had plenty of pastureland to graze their flocks as they followed the Euphrates River.

The Lord certainly knew Abraham needed an easy first step since the second leg of the journey would be much more difficult. God also knew Sarah needed this rather secure transition. It was going to be difficult enough for Abraham to handle the trauma of change in his own life without having to face a wife who was frustrated, insecure, and resistant to this step of faith.

Normal Temptations

The closer they came to Haran, the more Abraham was probably tempted to forget about God's call to Canaan. It's predictable that Terah would try to convince Abraham to forget the whole idea of crossing the burning desert and to stay in Haran. That's exactly what they did. But when Terah died, Abraham once again focused his thoughts on God's specific call. But he now faced the true test of faith. God was leading Abraham southwest of Haran and into a wilderness. He was heading to a place he had never been before.

Imagine the negative advice Abraham must have received from his relatives and the fifteen-year friends he was about to leave behind in Haran: "You're crazy, Abraham!" "You're out of your mind!" "There's nothing but a desert out there!" "You and your wife and servants will all die in that wasteland!" "You must have been dreaming when you received this so-called call from a strange god!"

An Insecure Wife

Considering what we know about most women, it doesn't take too much imagination to reconstruct what happened between Abraham and Sarah when he announced they were going to move on to Canaan. After fifteen years of security in Haran, the road ahead would frighten any normal woman, regardless of her spiritual and emotional maturity. Abraham not only faced pressure from his skeptical relatives, but he also faced the mood swings of an unhappy and insecure wife.

F. B. Meyer in his book on Abraham captured what may have happened: "And so the caravan started forth. The camels, heavily laden, attended by their drivers. The vast flocks mingling their bleatings with their drivers' cries. The demonstrative sorrow of eastern women mingling with the grave farewells of the men. The forebodings in many hearts of imminent danger and prospective disaster. Sarah may have even been broken down with bitter regrets."[2]

At this moment, it would have been easy for Abraham to give up the idea, to rationalize his partial obedience, to remain in Haran. But he didn't. As Meyer reminds us, he "faltered not. He staggered not through unbelief. He 'knew whom he had believed, and was persuaded that He was able to keep that which he had committed to Him against that day.' He was fully persuaded that what God had promised, He was able also to perform."[3]

God's Affirmation

At least four hundred miles lay ahead of Abraham and his family as they traveled across this monotonous wasteland, using their water supply sparingly. According to Josephus, they eventually arrived safely in a beautiful oasis, now called

Damascus. Even today a small village near Damascus is identified with Abraham's name.

How tempting it must have been for Abraham to settle in Damascus permanently, just as he had done in Haran. But this time Abraham kept his eyes fixed on the goal and his ears tuned to God's call that he had heard more than fifteen years before. He knew he had been sidetracked by his dearest and closest relative, his own father. He did not want that to happen again. Thus we read that he continued his journey and "came to the land of Canaan" (12:5, NASB).

God honored Abraham's faith and obedience as He always does for all of His children who follow Him fully. Once Abraham arrived in Canaan, the Lord appeared again and affirmed His divine promise: "To your descendants I will give this land" (12:7, NASB). As far as we know, this was the first word from God that Abraham had received since his initial encounter with the Lord in Ur a number of years before. However, even though God had been "silent," Abraham had been obedient.

Within the space of two verses we read that after Abraham had arrived in the land he "built an altar there to the LORD" (12:7–8, NASB). As he did, he was bearing witness to his new pagan neighbors that he and his family were different. They no longer made sacrifices to idols of wood or stone. Abraham had now made the complete transition from idolatry to worshiping the One true God.

Becoming God's Man Today

Principles to Live By

Principle 1. Once we begin to follow God, He is sympathetic to our human weaknesses and personal struggles.

The Lord knew it was a difficult decision for Abraham to leave his homeland, his relatives, and his family. Consequently, He demonstrated patience during the transition even though He knew that it would be better for Abraham in the long run to make a quick and clean break.

Just so, God often lets us learn lessons the hard way. He doesn't force us to do His perfect will. As only He can do, God often patiently waits for us to learn that His way is always best. Hopefully, we'll learn our lessons *before* it's too late to correct the situation and miss the blessings God wants us to experience.

In some instances, I'm convinced that the Lord bypasses us and uses someone else to achieve His special purposes in this world simply because we're not willing to go all the way to Canaan. Although we may not suffer any serious and overly painful consequences, we may live life less productively when it comes to "seeking first His kingdom and His righteousness." In fact, we may not even know the blessings we've missed until we stand before the judgment seat of Christ to receive the crowns and rewards that God has for His faithful children (2 Cor. 5:10; Phil. 3:12–14).

Principle 2. *Although God is understanding and patient when we walk out of His perfect will, He still disciplines those whom He loves.*

Even though Abraham was moving in the general direction of Canaan when he left Ur and headed for Haran, he still had not obeyed God's direct and specific command. He allowed his pagan father to take control, which resulted in delayed obedience. Although God allowed Abraham to remain in Haran, He eventually removed his father from the scene, which freed Abraham to continue on his journey. Furthermore, God did not speak to Abraham again and confirm His promise until he actually arrived in the land of Canaan, until he had obeyed completely.

Have you ever wondered why God doesn't seem to be real to you? Why He seems distant? At times, but not always, it's because we are trying to manipulate the Lord, to expect Him to guide and comfort us even though we are not living in full obedience.

Identifying with Abraham

Can you identify with Abraham's experience? I certainly can. There are times when I have disobeyed God, at least in some aspect of my life. Although I'm diligently doing a lot of things the Lord wants me to do, there may be one area where I'm deliberately walking out of His will. In my heart I know I'm being disobedient, but it's so easy to rationalize that this is an exception. "God understands," I say to myself. But the fact is, He's not pleased.

Does God leave me when this happens? Never. Rather, He simply allows me to reap what I sow, to be uncomfortable and out of fellowship with Him. He doesn't seem close to me. I have difficulty worshiping Him freely and wholeheartedly. Sometimes He allows me to face consequences and struggles I bring on myself because of my disobedience. What's the problem? It's me, my human weaknesses and my old flesh patterns.

Getting Back on Track

What is the solution? I must confess my sins and claim His ongoing forgiveness through the cleansing blood of Christ (1 John 1:9) and then once again follow God fully. I must continue my journey to Canaan.

Does this immediately solve the problem? In terms of forgiveness, yes. In terms of renewed fellowship with the Lord, it depends on the extent of my disobedience and what I've reaped in my life because of my disobedience. I've discovered that there's always some price to pay, even if it involves some lingering guilt in my ability to emotionally accept God's forgiveness. But how wonderful when I can once again hear His voice reassuring me of my intimate relationship with Him.

Principle 3. It is never too late to start obeying God, although we may need to obey Him within certain circumstances and parameters that were originally created by our disobedience.

In most instances, disobeying God can be corrected without suffering lifelong consequences. This was certainly true in Abraham's situation. His delayed obedience only delayed God's fullest blessing. That certainly happens many times in our Christian lives.

On the other hand, some decisions or actions we take out of the will of God can be disastrous. For example, if, as a Christian,

I violate God's will by deliberately marrying a non-Christian, it is virtually impossible to correct this kind of mistake other than through divorce. This may lead me to violate God's will a second time since divorce is not justified based solely on the fact that I am "unequally yoked." In this instance, God desires that I make the best of the situation by obeying His commands within this context, even though I may face lifelong problems in a relationship where we usually cannot agree on biblical and spiritual values for ourselves or for our children. [4]

Fortunately, most decisions we make out of God's will are not as complicated as the one I've just described. It is never too late to start obeying God. Remember, Abraham was seventy-five years old when he left Haran and got back in the center of God's perfect will.

Principle 4. Although Abraham's experiences give us power-ful principles to guide us in determining God's will today, we must not try to duplicate the specific ways or patterns God used to lead Abraham.

Many Christians make the mistake of expecting God to use the same methods in their lives that He used to reveal His will to some of these Old Testament greats, such as Abraham. This happens because we don't understand that God works in different ways at different times in history.

Prior to His written revelation in the Bible, God visibly appeared to certain individuals and spoke to them directly. There are many illustrations of this in both the Old and New Testaments. For example, He spoke to Moses through a burning bush (Exod. 3:1–4:17), and Jesus Christ spoke to the apostle Paul on the road to Damascus even before Paul became a Christian (Acts 9:1–9). Just so, Abraham represents an important beginning point in God's direct communication with mankind.

God's Will in His Word

Today, we have the divine record of these events and numerous directives and exhortations that specifically spell out God's will for our lives. In most instances, we need not wait for God to speak to determine His will. He has already spoken.

Let me illustrate. After Paul exhorted the Roman Christians to "test and approve what God's will is," he went on to outline in detailed fashion God's "good, pleasing and perfect will" (Rom. 12:2). For example, note the following directives that clearly outline God's will for all of us:

➤ For by the grace given me I say to every one of you: Do not think of yourself more highly than you ought, but rather think of yourself with sober judgment, in accordance with the measure of faith God has given you (Rom. 12:3).

➤ Love must be sincere. Hate what is evil; cling to what is good (12:9).

➤ Be devoted to one another in brotherly love. Honor one another above yourselves (12:10).

➤ Never be lacking in zeal, but keep your spiritual fervor, serving the Lord (12:11).

➤ Be joyful in hope, patient in affliction, faithful in prayer (12:12).

➤ Share with God's people who are in need. Practice hospitality (12:13).

➤ Bless those who persecute you; bless and do not curse (12:14).

➤ Rejoice with those who rejoice; mourn with those who mourn (12:15).

➤ Live in harmony with one another. Do not be proud, but be willing to associate with people of low position. Do not be conceited (12:16).

It's clear, even from these nine verses following Romans 12:1–2, that God clearly outlines much of His "good, pleasing and perfect will" in Scripture. But please don't misunderstand. God can do anything He wants to at any time. But direct revelations were unique, even in biblical history. Although God can certainly communicate directly today, we must be careful never to confuse what we think is God's voice with other voices that are vying for our attention.

Be Careful with Experience

It's dangerous to rely on experiences to determine God's will. Many impressions that we believe are coming from God may be coming right out of our own hearts, from our own selfish desires, things that *we* want to do. Furthermore, don't forget that Satan can appear as an angel of light. He is very subtle and is very effective at even using so-called Christian experiences to sidetrack believers.

"How can I be sure it's God speaking?" you ask. First, God can and does use experience. However, we must always evaluate our experiences and decisions in the light of the revealed Word of God. We must always ask: What has God already said? Does this idea, experience, or decision violate any aspect of the written Word of God? Remember also, it's important to determine whether our particular experience can be verified in Scripture with a similar experience. It's dangerous to decide that an experience is from the Holy Spirit if that experience is not described in Scripture. At this point, we also must be careful that we don't interpret and manipulate experiences in the Bible to make them fit our experiences. This too can lead to serious consequences.

Use Careful Biblical Interpretation

There's another error we must avoid. Some Christians use the Bible almost the same way others use experience. They look for a word from God in the Scriptures to determine His will.

But, you say, Isn't that what the Bible is for? The answer is yes, if we interpret Scripture accurately. But God never intended for us to take His statements out of context and give them meaning for our lives that does not reflect what He meant in the first place. This is why we must look for the principles from Scripture, divine guidelines that grow out of these biblical accounts that help us determine God's will in every aspect of our lives today. This is also why I've developed these application sections in these Old Testament character studies entitled Principles to Live By. Although God may not speak directly to us as He did to Abraham, He still speaks to us through his life and the lessons we can learn, lessons that can help us determine God's perfect will for our lives.

Personalizing These Principles

Are you having difficulty obeying God? You already know what He says you should do, but you also know you are violating His will, either totally or partially. If so, decide today that you are moving on toward Canaan. Don't be afraid to face the uncertainty of the future, even the burning desert. If what God is calling you to do is clear in His Word, He will honor your decision.

Set a Goal

As you evaluate the principles we've learned from Abraham's experience thus far, select the principle you feel you need to focus on the most. For example, perhaps you rely too heavily on subjective experiences in determining the will of God rather than on the objective Word of God. Or perhaps you are punishing yourself for some mistake you've made in the past, even though you've confessed your sin. Remember that God has forgiven you and wants you to go forward in your Christian life with a free conscience.

Whatever principle you choose, write out a specific goal to help you apply that principle in your life:

_____

_____

_____

_____

Memorize the Following Scripture

Commit the following Scripture to memory to help you realize your goal:

> *Instead, speaking the truth in love, we will in all things grow up into him who is the Head, that is, Christ. From him the whole body, joined and held together by every supporting ligament, grows and builds itself up in love, as each part does its work.*
> EPHESIANS 4:15–16

Growing Together

The following questions are designed for small-group discussion:

1. How have you experienced God's patience when you have walked out of His will in some aspect of your life?

2. How do you keep from rationalizing your behavior, convincing yourself that what you're doing is God's will for you even though the Word of God does not condone what you're doing?

3. How has God disciplined you to bring you back into His will?

4. In what ways have you found yourself punishing yourself rather than accepting God's forgiveness?

5. Can you share an experience where you felt God was speaking to you and found out later that it was purely your own personal desire to do something?

6. What can we pray for you specifically?

Chapter 3
_____

Abraham's Plan "Goes South"
Read Genesis 12:10–20

*H*ave you ever felt great about your relationship with God and suddenly the bottom drops out? You've committed your life to the Lord, to follow Him fully, and then everything seemed to go south.

Welcome to the Christian Club. It's not a new experience. Just when you think everything is in order spiritually, you face a crisis, in reality, a test of faith. It happened to Abraham shortly after he obeyed God fully and crossed the burning desert into Canaan. It happened after God appeared to him and affirmed the promise that He would give Abraham this new land (Gen. 12:7). It happened after Abraham responded in worship by building an altar to the Lord (12:7–8). The crisis came quickly and abruptly. We simply read: "Now there was a *famine* in the land" (12:10).

Lord, What's Happening?

As far as we know, Abraham had never faced a famine before, not in Ur nor in Haran, which were both prosperous and productive areas. Imagine what must have gone through his mind. "I came all the way out here for this? Lord, I obeyed you fully. I thought this was to be a land of blessings!" Think about the complaining he must have encountered from those closest to him. "Abraham, I told you that you were out of your mind to come way out here! So you obeyed your God! For what reason? So He could bring us all out here in the wilderness to destroy us?"

What irony. After this huge caravan had made it all the way across the burning desert, Abraham now faced the danger of being totally wiped out—man and beast—in the midst of the land that God had promised would provide him with blessings.

Most of us tend to act quickly under pressure, especially when our human needs are not being met and doubly so when we're under pressure from others. Abraham faced both problems.

Abraham took quick action. We read: "So Abram went down to Egypt to sojourn there, for the famine was severe in the land" (12:10, NASB). Abraham literally went south, well, to be exact, southwest. When the bottom dropped out, he wasted no time doing something about it.

Egypt—A Place of Refuge

Over the years, Egypt has become a place of survival and refuge for God's children. Many years later, Joseph's brothers sold him into Egypt where he eventually became prime minister. Through this experience, God used Joseph to provide food for his brothers and aging father when they too faced a famine in Canaan (42:1–2). Centuries later Egypt also became a refuge for Jesus Christ when Herod attempted to snuff out His life (Matt. 2:13).

It's not surprising then that Abraham sought refuge for his family. But attempting to save them from starvation was not Abraham's essential problem. Unfortunately, he took matters into his own hands without consulting God, the One who brought him into the land in the first place. In other words, Abraham made a man-centered decision.

If Abraham had looked to God for specific instructions during this crisis, it's possible that God would have sent him to

Egypt anyway but with a specific strategy on how to face the problems that he would encounter when he got there. It's also possible that God had other plans for Abraham.

Think of the creative alternatives. When God wants to meet our needs miraculously there is no limit to what He can do. How about providing water out of the rocks? What about manna from heaven or quail from the sea? (Exod. 16; Num. 11:31.) How about barrels of meal that never run dry? (1 Kings 17.)

In future years He would do things like this many times for the children of Israel as they left Egypt and journeyed through the wilderness. Had Abraham allowed God to perform these miracles, think of the testimony it would have been to the pagan Canaanites who no doubt were laughing up their sleeves at this strange wanderer who claimed to have access to the one true God.

It appears that Abraham did not give God the opportunity to display His mighty power. Rather, he acted on his own, choosing what he believed was the only alternative. He went down to Egypt.

Leaving One Crisis to Face Another

When Abraham arrived in Egypt, he faced another crisis. Egyptian royalty were on the lookout for beautiful women. If the women were married and their husbands resisted, warriors would simply murder the husband and take the wife captive to serve in their masters' harems. Since Sarah was a very desirable woman, even at age sixty-five, Abraham was worried and rightly so.

If Paul's account in Romans 1 describes the world of Abraham's day—which I believe it does—mankind in general had totally deteriorated. Abraham was no fool. He knew what motivated these men. Consequently, he devised a plan to protect himself. "As he was about to enter Egypt, he said to his wife Sarai, 'I know what a beautiful woman you are. When the Egyptians see you, they will say, "This is his wife." Then they will kill me but will let you live. Say you are my sister, so that I will be treated well for your sake and my life will be spared because of you'" (Gen. 12:11–13).

Abraham's plan was based on a rather intriguing rationalization. Sarah was his *half-sister* (11:29; 20:12). She was the daughter of his father but not the daughter of his mother. So Abraham's statement to the Egyptians was a half-truth. Sarah *was* his sister, but she was also his wife (20:12).

Pharaoh's Trophy Wife

When Abraham and Sarah crossed the border into Egypt, Pharaoh's spies quickly spotted Sarah. Her natural beauty plus her distinctive foreign features made her an easy target for money-hungry men who were also working hard for some special favor with the king of Egypt. Furthermore, it's a fact of history that Egyptian men were not as attracted to Egyptian women as much as they were attracted to women outside of their own culture. Insensitive and selfish, they believed their own women faded early. As much as we detest this kind of male thinking, it's was the reality of Abraham's day.[1] Unfortunately, we see this happening in American culture when an older man divorces his lifetime mate and marries a younger woman we often refer to as a trophy wife.

Playing the Game

Pharaoh wasted little time responding to the report. We read, "And when Pharaoh's officials saw her, they praised her to Pharaoh, and she was taken into his palace" (12:15).

Since Abraham had designed the plan ahead of time, he offered no resistance and neither did Sarah. They both cooperated fully, which pleased Pharaoh, who rewarded Abraham with "sheep and cattle, male and female donkeys, menservants and maidservants and camels" (12:16). Evidently, Sarah did all she could to play the game since Pharaoh "treated Abram well for her sake" (12:16).

For many of us, it's difficult to understand Abraham's reasoning. His strong desire to save his own life, which was his basic motive, made him willing to give up his wife. But if you also take into consideration Abraham's spiritual immaturity and his cultural background, it's not difficult to understand his thinking and his actions. Let's not forget that Sarah came straight out of the same pagan environment as Abraham. Her morals were not based on God's laws, as we'll see when she later offered her maidservant to Abraham to bear the promised son.

Let's not be smug about all this. Think of the twentieth-century men we read about daily who are caught in acts of deception, deceit, adultery, desertion, and even murder. Businessmen sport their trophy wives, and sadly some of today's sexually oriented crimes are being committed by men in some of the highest levels of our government. As I write this, one of our prominent senators has been relieved of his duties because of numerous accounts of sexual harassment.

Let us not forget that some men who claim to be God's servants are guilty as well. Think for a moment about the scandals that have broken out among some of our prominent television evangelists. In many respects, we're no different in our heart of hearts in spite of our Hebrew-Christian traditions.

A Serious Mistake

As we've seen, there are several reasons why Abraham did what he did. But his actions were not right. He made a serious mistake. Had he consulted the Lord, he may have been the first man God used to convey a powerful message to the Egyptians, that God exists and desires to reach out to all men. Rather than falling on these people in judgment, which God eventually did, He might have extended His grace through Abraham.

You see, if Abraham had allowed God to prepare the way for him in Egypt, his strategy would have been God-centered rather than man-centered. However, Abraham was operating under his own steam and had been ever since he headed for Egypt to avoid the famine in Canaan. But God in His grace, as He so often does throughout Old Testament history, stepped in to bail Abraham out of his predicament.

God's Patience and Faithfulness

God's patience and faithfulness in the lives of His children is often amazing and encouraging (12:17–13:4). This is particularly true when He selects someone to achieve a special purpose. No purpose was more special than the salvation of the world. This is a primary reason God chose Abraham.

In spite of Abraham's failures, God brought judgment upon Pharaoh for his sins (12:17). We read that "the LORD inflicted serious diseases on Pharaoh and his household because of Abram's wife Sarai" (12:17).

Somehow Pharaoh discovered the full truth, and he wasted no time in calling Abraham into his court. Face to face with this wandering nomad, he asked some penetrating questions and then issued an order: "'What have you done to me?' he said. 'Why didn't you tell me she was your wife? Why did you say, "She is my sister," so that I took her to be my wife? Now then, here is your wife. Take her and go!'" (12:18–19).

We see God's amazing grace when Abraham was allowed to keep the servants and animals that Pharaoh had given him in exchange for Sarah. To top it off, Pharaoh's men escorted Abraham out of Egypt and back to Canaan where he belonged. Ironically, God used pagan people to get His servant back on the right track (12:20).

Another Lesson Learned

Abraham seems to have learned his lesson well. When he returned to the place where he had first built an altar, he once again "called on the name of the LORD" (13:3–4). This, of course, is what he should have done in the first place.

Again, let's remember that this man was just a beginner in his walk with God. Calling on the name of the Lord and worshiping Him was a totally new experience for this man who had for most of his life bowed to idols of wood and stone. In those initial years, both Abraham *and* Sarah made some serious mistakes. But what is so encouraging, God patiently helped this couple to learn from those mistakes.

Becoming God's Man Today

Principles to Live By

Abraham didn't do as well as he might have in ascertaining God's will when he was faced with a major crisis. But how would you and I have responded if we had been Abraham? More importantly, can we discover God's will today and avoid Abraham's mistakes? There are at least four significant lessons we can learn from Abraham's life and his decision to go down to Egypt.

Principle 1. *We will face periodic crises in our Christian lives, even when we are following God fully.*

Although it's not pleasant, this is the only way most of us grow spiritually. We tend to stand still when we don't face struggles and problems. Let's expect them. Remember that some of these crises are tests God allows in our lives because He wants to teach us and to prepare us for an even greater work for Him.

Natural Circumstances

Other crises come because of the natural circumstances of life. Let's remember that the principle of sin is at work in this world. As Christians we are victims of the environment in which we live. We must expect difficulties—physically, mentally, and spiritually. Let's remember that we are not yet glorified. We are still living in this body that has also been affected by sin (Phil. 1:22). It's at times like this we must remember the words of the apostle Paul who wrote to the Corinthians: "Now we know that if the earthly tent we live in is destroyed, we have a building from God, an eternal house in heaven, not built by human hands. Meanwhile we groan, longing to be clothed with our heavenly dwelling" (2 Cor. 5:1–2).

Disobedience

However, one of the greatest lessons we can learn from Abraham is that we often face crises when we are out of God's will. Thankfully, the Lord wants to graciously and lovingly bring us back to Canaan. Although this is often a painful experience, it demonstrates God's loving discipline in our lives.

At this point, be careful. Because of His faithfulness, God will at times continue to pour out blessings on us in spite of our disobedience, just as He did for Abraham. At that moment, our tendency is to rationalize and to continue to dabble in the world, to continue to violate His will as it is revealed in His Word. Because of God's grace, the results of this kind of sinful behavior are not immediate. But ultimately God will discipline us because He loves us. Perhaps one of the greatest prices we pay for disobedience will come a full generation later when we see our children grow up and follow our own self-centered behavior, becoming just like us or even worse.

A Sad Story

I'm thinking of a man I know whose father is a well-known pastor, at least in some circles. It's common knowledge that this father is living a double life and covering it up. Sadly, he has duped many of the people he ministers to into buying into his hypocritical lies. Because of the power structure he has set up to protect himself, it's virtually impossible for people to confront him, even with serious evidence regarding his immoral and unethical lifestyle.

This son has grown up to be just like his father. In fact, his sins are even greater than his father's. I'm reminded of Ahab who became king of Israel and made the sins of Jeroboam seem almost trivial.

The story doesn't end here. Most of this father's children have followed suit and have walked out of the will of God. One of his daughters, whom I know well, has completely abandoned her own family to commit some of the same sins. I'll never forget her remark to me one day when she said, "The thing I hate the most in my father is the very thing I'm doing myself."

What a price to pay for disobedience. We may seemingly get by with our sin, but ultimately, we'll face severe discipline, if not in our own lives, in the lives of our children. That is a terrible price to pay.

Principle 2. *When we face crises, we will always be tempted to go to extremes in solving our problems.*

God honors sound thinking and responsible actions. However, we can easily get into trouble because of the ego satisfaction we enjoy when we work out our problems all by ourselves. On the other hand, because we often tend to be insecure and afraid of making decisions, we may withdraw and fail to fulfill our human responsibility. It's difficult but necessary to maintain a balance between these two extremes.

There's no question as to which extreme Abraham went when he faced the famine in Canaan. This is really the most common error we make as men. We're often ego-driven and fail to consult God for help. In most instances this will lead us into serious trouble. One thing is certain. When this happens, we won't experience God's greatest blessings in our lives.

Principle 3. *God's faithfulness and patience continues in our lives no matter what our decisions.*

This is true because God has called us to be His children. He has given us eternal life. He has promised never to leave us nor forsake us. Again, our temptation is to interpret God's faithfulness and blessings as a confirmation that He is not displeased with our behavior.

How easy it is to rationalize: "I'm making even more money than before." "I really feel good and secure about this decision. I'm really enjoying this relationship." "If God were really displeased, He would certainly stop using me in the lives of others."

How deceptive emotions or circumstances can be. We must never take advantage of God's love and grace. Ultimately, we will reap what we sow.

Principle 4. We must follow God's divine order in determining His will for our lives.

Consult God

Based upon what we already know about God's communication with Abraham, he probably could have gotten word directly from God by asking what to do in the midst of the famine in Canaan. When we're facing crises, we too can consult God, particularly through the Word that He has already revealed to us. We must consult the Scriptures carefully for the directives and principles that will guide us in doing His will. When making a decision, we must always ask: Is there anything in God's revealed Word, the Bible, that would teach us that this is a right or wrong decision?

We must be careful, however, that we don't use the Bible as a magic book. For example, some Christians let the Scriptures fall open to a certain place, allowing their eyes to fall on a certain verse, and then take that verse out of context and use it to make a decision. That is a violation of the sound-mind principle we find in Scripture (2 Tim. 1:7).

God wants us to examine the Scriptures regularly to discover His will (Acts 17:11). The psalmist says that a wise man delights in the law of the Lord and "on his law he meditates day and night" (Ps. 1:2). It is primarily the revealed Word of God that directs us in our lives today. In this sense we have a great advantage over Abraham who only heard from God periodically.

But, you ask, Can't we consult God directly? The answer is yes, since James wrote: "If any of you lacks wisdom, he should ask God, who gives generously to all without finding fault, and it will be given to him" (James 1:5). However, we should always combine this kind of prayer with a study of Scripture since the Word of God is filled with divine wisdom. Furthermore, should we believe we have received wisdom directly from God, we must always check that wisdom against the teachings of Scripture. Any thought or idea that contradicts the Word of God cannot be from God.

Consult Other Mature Christians

At this point, we have another unique advantage over Abraham for he had no one else to turn to but God. In his day, there was "no one righteous, not even one." No one understood the will of God and no one was seeking after God. The apostle Paul, quoting the psalmist said, "Their throats are open graves; their tongues practice deceit. The poison of vipers is on their lips. Their mouths are full of cursing and bitterness." And, "there is no fear of God before their eyes" (Rom. 3:13–14, 18).

Today we not only have the Scriptures, but most of us are surrounded by mature Christians who can assist us and help us determine the will of God. This principle of consulting other mature members of the body of Christ is illustrated throughout the New Testament. Note some of the following exhortations:

> ➤ Let the word of Christ dwell in you richly as you teach and admonish one another with all wisdom. (Col. 3:16)

> ➤ And let us consider how we may spur one another on toward love and good deeds. (Heb. 10:24)

> ➤ But encourage one another daily, as long as it is called Today, so that none of you may be hardened by sin's deceitfulness. (Heb. 3:13)

The functioning body of Christ is one of the most wonderful realities that came into being on the Day of Pentecost. Jesus Christ is the head of the church. And "from Him the whole body, joined and held together by every supporting ligament, grows and builds itself up in love, *as each part does its work*" (Eph. 4:16).

Observe Circumstances Carefully

We must ask ourselves the following questions: Does it make good sense? Is it logical and rational? Is there an overall pattern? What will happen if I make this decision? What are the ultimate advantages for me and my family? What are the ultimate disadvantages? Most importantly, how will this decision affect my spiritual life and my maturity?

Circumstances *are* important in determining God's will. Sometimes God wants us to circumvent these circumstances through sound thinking. But sometimes He wants us to stand still and see what He will do. But always He wants us to consult Him through His Word and through prayer and seek advice and wisdom from other mature Christians whom we trust. When we follow this procedure, more often than not, we will gain insight regarding what to do, particularly in making decisions where the Scriptures are silent.

Be Cautious About Feelings

It's not wrong to consider how we feel when we're attempting to make a decision, but we must be exceedingly careful. Imagine for a moment what would have happened if Jesus Christ had based His decision to go to the cross purely on His emotions. He probably would not have followed through, and understandably so. The inward pain Jesus felt in the garden of Gethsemane was so intense that His perspiration fell to the ground as drops of blood. He prayed that the cup of suffering and death that He had to drink would be removed. But His final words to the Father are a guideline to us all, "Yet not my will, but yours be done" (Luke 22:42).

Emotion can be a very deceptive element in decision-making. Yet our human tendency is to put our feelings at the top of the list rather than at the bottom.

Any decision that involves uncertainty—and most do—creates negative feelings. For years, psychologists have recognized this element in the decision-making process as approach-avoidance conflicts and ambivalent feelings. It's a part of being human. Like the proverbial headache, both Christians and non-Christians experience these negative emotions.

These mixed feelings are very predictable. When we are making an important decision, particularly in a crisis, we'll always experience positive and negative feelings simultaneously. Furthermore, the closer we come to making the decision, the stronger the negative emotions become. The farther away we get from making the decision, the stronger the positive emotions become, which in turn makes the decision easier to think about.

I've seen the problem of ambivalence particularly in the lives of older single people. The farther they are away from a decision to marry, the more comfortable they become about the prospect. But the closer they get to saying "I do," the stronger the negative emotions become.

At a distance, they are able to see all of the positive advantages of being married—love, security, a home, children, etc. But the closer they come to the decision, the negative emotions become more intense regarding greater responsibility, loss of certain freedoms, the possibility of failure, etc.

Unfortunately, many Christians equate these emotional dynamics with the leadership of the Holy Spirit. When they have negative feelings, they believe that the Holy Spirit is saying no. They feel He has taken away their peace of mind and heart.

On the other hand, when they have positive feelings, they feel the Holy Spirit is saying yes, giving them peace of heart and mind. The main problem with this approach to decision-making is that it makes the Holy Spirit ambivalent and unstable. The truth is that God never wavers when it comes to His will, but we do.

The same emotional dynamics surround most every decision we make—vocational choices, where to go to school, where to go to church, where to invest money, how to spend money, where to live, etc. Consequently, we must beware of relying on our emotions. They will deceive us. In fact, many decisions have to be made in spite of negative emotions because we know it is the right thing to do.

Personalizing These Principles

The following questions will help you personalize the lessons we've just learned from Abraham's decision to leave Canaan and go to Egypt:

1. How do I react when crises come into my life even though I'm attempting to do all I can to follow God fully?

2. Do I distinguish between crises that are normal and natural because of the realities of life and those that happen because I'm walking out of the will of God?

3. Am I rationalizing my disobedience because I'm not experiencing God's immediate discipline in my life?

4. To what extent do I maintain a balance in decision-making by not going to extremes, on the one hand, relying on my own strengths and skills, and, on the other hand, simply relying on God and neglecting my God-ordained human responsibility?

5. To what extent am I following God's divine order in determining His will for my life?

Step 1: Consulting the Scriptures.

Step 2: Consulting other mature Christians, remembering that "in the multitude of counselors there is safety" (Prov. 11:14b, KJV).

Step 3: Evaluating circumstances in my environment carefully but not allowing them to control my decision.

Step 4: Not allowing my feelings and emotions to overly determine what is a wise or unwise decision.

Set a Goal

As you read over the principles outlined in this chapter and ask yourself the questions just outlined, what particular area should you give attention to in your attempt to determine the will of God? For example, perhaps you are relying too heavily on your emotions, how you feel about a particular situation. Or perhaps you allow circumstances to defeat you, to keep you from developing an adequate strategy to circumvent these circumstances. On the other hand, you may be the kind of person who never says die! You always try to overcome circumstances, not realizing that God may want you to spend more time seeking His will through the study of the Word of God and in prayer. Whatever your particular need, develop a personal goal:

_____

_____

_____

_____

Memorize the Following Scripture

Commit the following Scripture to memory to help you realize your goal:

> *Blessed is the man who does not walk in the counsel of the wicked or stand in the way of sinners or sit in the seat of mockers. But his delight is in the law of the LORD, and on his law he meditates day and night.*
>
> PSALM 1:1–2

Growing Together

The following questions are designed for small-group discussion:

1. Would you be willing to share a particular crisis situation in your own life where you feel that you've violated one of the principles we've studied when you made a particular decision? If so, would you mind sharing the results of your decision?

2. What particular crisis are you struggling with at present? Would you allow us to share our own experiences to help you with your decision?

3. Do you have an experience in decision-making that you could share with us where you have violated the Lord's divine sequence in determining the will of God? For example, you may not have consulted the Word of God

adequately. Or you may have relied too much on your own abilities to handle the circumstances. Or you may have made this decision on your own. Or you may have relied too much on how you felt about the situation. Share what happened because you violated this divine sequence at some point along the way.

4. Do you have any specific areas where you are making decisions that you can share with us for prayer?

Chapter 4

A Skeleton in the Closet
Read Genesis 13:1–18

More than we'd like to admit, many of us have skeletons in our closets—a decision, an event, an act, a memory from the past that may suddenly haunt us in the present. In some instances it's a skeleton that we've created. For others it's in our closet because someone else placed it there—a parent, a marital partner, a friend, or some circumstance beyond our control, such as a natural disaster.

For some, this skeleton is a minor irritation that appears periodically. For others, it may be grotesque or frightening and quite visible every time we open our closet door.

Then there's the skeleton that we hardly recognize anymore. But when circumstances are just right, the closet door swings open and there it hangs. Unfortunately, Abraham had this kind of skeleton in his closet. As we read his life story, it's so well camouflaged, we hardly notice it. But it was there and clearly visible. In fact, Abraham's skeleton was alive and well. It was his nephew, Lot.

Leave Your Father's Household

When Abraham received a call to leave Ur of the Chaldees (Gen. 12:1), God instructed him to leave, not only his country and his *own household*, but also *all his relatives* (12:1). His failure to make a complete break with his father resulted in at least a fifteen-year delay in going to Canaan. But when he was on his way once again, his failure to leave his nephew, Lot, in Haran complicated his life even more.

Why did God want Abraham to make such a complete break with those closest to him? Wasn't he to be a blessing to *all nations?* Why not begin with his father and his brother's son?

God is omniscient. He knows the deepest thoughts and intents of our hearts now and forever. He knew that Terah would deter Abraham from continuing on to Canaan once they had reached Haran. He also knew that Lot would create problems for Abraham once they settled in the land.

Lot had a worldly heart. His motives were selfish. Lot was this kind of man when they left Ur. He was this kind of man when they left Haran fifteen years later. This is the kind of man he would continue to be. God foresaw what would happen, and He preferred to spare Abraham the problems he would face in Canaan.

On the other hand, God also knew there were certain lessons Abraham could learn from his failure to follow His will in every detail. As always, God is able to take our sins and make them work together for our good. This, of course, never justifies our mistakes, but demonstrates that God's ways are so far beyond our ways that we can only accept this kind of antinomy by faith.

When tension rose between Abraham and Lot, it was not a surprise to God. However, Abraham seemed totally caught off-guard. Although he probably knew Lot's character was seriously flawed, he overlooked his nephew's worldly nature and even felt a sense of responsibility for his welfare. Or Lot may have also been on his best behavior—for a time. But what he was in his heart and always had been suddenly came to the surface after they had returned from Egypt.

Shared Blessings

God was not out to get Lot. Although He knew this man's heart, as He knows every man's heart, God wanted him to change. Just as He wanted Abraham to follow Him fully, so He wanted Lot and his family to walk in His perfect will. Consequently, He blessed Lot with flocks and herds and tents, just as He blessed Abraham (13:5). In fact, when Abraham received sheep, oxen, donkeys, and servants from Pharaoh, he probably shared these gifts with Lot. If so, Lot too cashed in on Abraham's Egyptian bonanza. God's gifts to Abraham resulted in His blessings on Lot. It's not uncommon for ungodly children and relatives to share in the grace God bestows on godly parents and grandparents.

Why would Abraham share this wealth with Lot? Was it simply that he was generous and unselfish? To answer these questions, put yourself in his place. Remember that Abraham fell into enormous wealth through his own self-centered strategy that left God out of the picture. He certainly hadn't forgotten that he gave up his wife to a licentious and evil king to save his own skin. Consequently, he may have felt guilty—just as you and I would—when he received such a generous gift from the Pharaoh in spite of his own selfish decision. Sharing this ill-gotten gain with Lot may have been his attempt to alleviate his own guilt, to compensate for what he had done wrong.

Even though Abraham may have been operating out of a sense of guilt, in many respects he was also a sensitive and unselfish person. In spite of his weaknesses, he had character qualities that Lot did not. Perhaps this is another reason why God chose Abraham out of his idolatrous environment to be the channel through whom He would bring the savior into the world. This is not to say that Abraham was saved by his works. In spite of Abraham's idolatrous lifestyle, God may have seen remnants of righteous acts in Abraham's heart and life, character qualities that enabled Abraham to respond to God's mercy, grace, and sovereign call on His life. Again we have a divine mystery that is irreconcilable from our limited perspective.

The Skeleton Appears

Abraham and Lot both became rich men (13:6–7). The Scriptures state that Abraham "had become *very wealthy* in livestock and in silver and gold" (13:2). Likewise, "Lot . . . also had flocks and herds and tents" (13:5). Even though there was plenty of vacant land (13:9), their "possessions were so great that they were not able to stay together" (13:6). Ironically, the land could not support them (13:6–7). Consequently, serious strife broke out between Abraham's and Lot's herdsmen (13:7).

Wealth is both a curse and a blessing. Even those with great wisdom have difficulty keeping unhappiness, jealousy, and feuding away from the door. There will always be those in the family structure who have carnal and selfish attitudes.

Abraham's wealth got him into trouble rather early in his walk with God. Although his own attitudes were right, he had no way of transferring his perspectives to those who worked for him, nor was he able to control Lot's self-centered behavior and those who worked for Lot. Consequently, Abraham's herdsmen fought and feuded with Lot's herdsmen over who used what pastures and what water holes and where they would erect their tents. Ironically, this quarreling wasn't caused by crowded conditions per se. Later, Abraham reminded Lot there was plenty of space, so why fight? (13:9).

A Magnanimous Offer

Abraham offered a solution to this problem that revealed his heart. "Let's not have any quarreling between you and me," he said, "or between your herdsmen and mine for we are brothers. Is not the whole land before you?" (13:8–9).

Abraham was wise enough to know that they had no choice but to part company, and yet he made Lot a magnanimous offer. "If you go to the left," he said, then, "I'll go to the right; if you go to the right, I'll go to the left" (13:9). Abraham knew this was the only way unity could be restored between them.

What an unselfish, generous spirit. Abraham certainly knew that God had blessed Lot because of him. Yet he was willing to put Lot on an equal footing, to offer him a choice that could definitely allow his nephew to end up with a better deal.

In making this offer, Abraham was not naive in terms of what the stakes were. He knew what lay eastward toward Jordan, a virtual "garden of the LORD" (13:10). He was well aware he might end up with the least desirable land. But his love for Lot, his desire for unity and peace, and his concern about his personal witness in a pagan community seemed more important to Abraham than his own material welfare. Abraham was still a long way from where he ought to be spiritually, but at this moment in his life he was not the man he once was.

A Selfish Choice

The moment Lot had a choice, the moment Abraham gave him an opportunity to make a decision on his own, his true character surfaced (13:10–12). He "looked up and saw that the whole plain of the Jordan was well watered, like the garden of the LORD, like the land of Egypt, toward Zoar" (13:10).

Problems often begin with our eyes. It's what we *see* that leads us to make wrong decisions. How true this was of Lot. Furthermore, his Egyptian experience that resulted in greater possessions predictably stimulated a taste for more and better.

What a familiar scenario. Lot's material wealth combined with a selfish heart made him vulnerable and susceptible to being even more selfish. Sadly, his choice would also have a very negative effect on him and his whole family. He was about to become even more deeply rooted in the things of the world. He chose to move toward the city of Sodom, one of the most degenerate cities in the world at that time. If Lot was aware of this fact, it didn't deter him from making this selfish and carnal decision. The Scriptures speak for themselves: "So Lot chose for himself the whole plain of the Jordan and set out toward the east. The two men parted company: Abram lived in the land of Canaan, while Lot lived among the cities of the plain and pitched his tents near Sodom. Now the men of Sodom were wicked and were sinning greatly against the LORD" (13:11–13).

Reassurance

Abraham received his first revelation when God called him to leave Ur, to "go to the *land* I will show you" (12:1). When he eventually arrived in Canaan, God appeared to Abraham again, this time giving him "more light" on his path, reassuring him he was *in* the land and he would receive it as God had promised, not only for himself but also for his offspring (12:7).

Faith Becomes Sight

After Abraham had unselfishly given Lot the best part of the promised land, God became even more specific in His revelation and told Abraham that his unselfishness would be rewarded many times over:

> The LORD said to Abram after Lot had parted from him, "Lift up your eyes from where you are and look north and south, east and west. All the land that you see I will give to you and your offspring forever. I will make your offspring like the dust of the earth, so that if anyone could count the dust, then your offspring could be counted. Go, walk through the length and breadth of the land, for I am giving it to you." (Gen. 13:14–17)

God wanted Abraham to know that compared with what his descendants would receive, he hadn't really given up very much. With every step of obedience, Abraham experienced more light and greater reassurance. Although he stepped out by *faith*, not knowing where he was going, he could now *see* what God had in mind. He could feel the sand between his toes as he walked through the promised land from one end to the other.

In Losing We Win

This should not surprise us because this is the way God frequently leads us. The more we do His will, the more we can understand regarding His plan for our lives. Although our journey may be marked by famine and even painful encounters with those closest to us, God has our best interests at heart.

Even when we seem to lose, we will win. This should be reassuring for every Christian who is struggling to make a decision based on unselfish motives.

Obviously, Abraham at this moment in his life didn't clearly understand the meaning of all that God had revealed to him. He certainly didn't comprehend the eternal aspects of this marvelous promise. But there would come a time when he would understand more completely. Listen to the author of Hebrews as he reflects on this man's life, helping us to understand more fully what Abraham was thinking: "By faith he [Abraham] made his home in the promised land like a stranger in a foreign country; he lived in tents, as did Isaac and Jacob, who were heirs with him of the same promise. For he was looking forward to the city with foundations, whose architect and builder is God" (Heb. 11:9–10).

Becoming God's Man Today

Principles to Live By

All of us have skeletons in our closets, some are big and some are small, some are difficult to live with and some are hardly worth mentioning. Some of these skeletons are there because of our own wrongdoing; others are there because of the wrongdoing of others. As we think about the principles that come from this aspect of Abraham's life, let's focus on the decisions we've made in the past that periodically, or regularly, haunt us in the present. How should we as Christians handle our skeletons?

Principle 1. We should always remember that God's forgiveness in Christ extends to everything we've done in the past.

If you're a Christian, you need not allow skeletons in your closet to defeat you and keep you in a state of worry and concern. Believe the great truth that John wrote in his first epistle: "If we confess our sins, he is faithful and just and will forgive us our sins and purify us from all unrighteousness" (1 John 1:9).

Paul gave us another great truth in his second letter to the Corinthians: "Therefore, if anyone is in Christ, he is a new creation; the old has gone, the new has come!" (2 Cor. 5:17).

Even though we are still living in this body and subject to failure—and will be until Christ comes again—we should view ourselves and other Christians as God views us. We have been made perfect in Christ. This should be our message to others. Not only has God reconciled us to himself through Christ, but He has given us the ministry of reconciliation (2 Cor. 5:19). We can and should share with others what a wonderful and glorious identity and position they can have in Christ if they accept His message of love and grace.

Principle 2. Although God sees us as new creations in Christ, it does not mean we have in actuality new bodies and new souls.

Some Christians seem to think that to be in Christ means that everything becomes new the moment we receive Christ. Not so. The Scriptures certainly do not teach this and the evidence confirms the fact that we don't have new bodies or new souls the moment we receive Jesus Christ as personal Lord and Savior.

Paul spoke to this issue clearly in the very context in which he stated that if we're in Christ, we are new creations: "Now we know that if the earthly tent [body] we live in is destroyed, we have a building from God, an eternal house in heaven, not built by human hands. Meanwhile *we groan,* longing to be clothed with our heavenly dwelling" (2 Cor. 5:1–2).

The body and soul (our intellect, our emotions, and our will) are inseparably linked while we live on this earth. They represent both the material and immaterial part of our being. What happens to the body affects the soul and what happens to the soul affects the body.

This is why we use the term *psychosomatic* when we discuss illnesses that are both body and mind related. The Greek words *psuche* (meaning "soul") and *soma* (meaning "body") are used together to form this one word in English.

All people—Christians and non-Christians—manifest psychosomatic symptoms under certain circumstances. That's why the Proverb reads, "Pleasant words are a honeycomb, sweet to the *soul* and healing to the *bones*" (Prov. 16:24). In other words, we can make people feel good all over, in both mind and body, with pleasant, kind, and reassuring words. Conversely, we can make people feel bad with sarcasm and comments that reflect anger and insensitivity.

This is why Paul told us to "encourage each other with *these words*" (1 Thess. 4:18), that is, the good news regarding the fact that when Christians die before Christ comes, they go to be with the Lord. At that point in time, the Christian's "body" and "soul" *do* separate, which is something only God can cause to happen (2 Cor. 5:6). The soul, the real person, enters God's presence. The body decays and returns to dust. This separation, however, is only temporary until we *all*— those who died in Christ and those who are still alive in Christ when He comes again—receive a brand new body that will never perish (1 Cor. 15:51–53; 1 Thess. 4:16–17). At that time, our soul, which has already been perfected by the Lord when we enter His presence (or the moment we are raptured), will be united to a perfect body that is like the glorified body of our Lord Jesus Christ.

A New Identity

What happens when we receive Christ? We are born again by the Holy Spirit (John 3:3; Titus 3:5). Some believe that our spirit, which they say has been dead to this point in time, becomes alive and new. Personally, I believe it is difficult to distinguish between the soul and the spirit and to explain actually what happens at conversion. But one thing is very certain, we have a new identity in Jesus Christ. As far as God is concerned, we are *totally* new for He sees us as already raised up with Christ and "seated . . . with him in the heavenly realms" (Eph. 2:6). From God's perspective, we are already glorified (Rom. 8:30). In other words, we have a new body and a brand-new soul and spirit. He does not look at our past lives and what we have done that is out of His will. We are truly forgiven.

A New Capacity and Ability

Not only do we receive a new identity in Christ, but we also receive a new capacity and ability to become more and more like Jesus Christ. Again, some believe this new capacity relates to our reborn spirit that was once dead. Whatever happens, it's clear from Scripture that we have the divine resources, God's indwelling Spirit who gives us power to put off our old self and put on our new self which is "created to be like God in true righteousness and holiness" (Eph. 4:22–24).

This is why Paul prayed as he did for the Ephesian Christians:

> I pray that out of his glorious riches he may strengthen you with power *through his Spirit in your inner being,* so that Christ may dwell in your hearts through faith. And I pray that you, being rooted and established in love, may have power, together with all the saints, to grasp how wide and long and high and deep is the love of Christ, and to know this love that surpasses knowledge—that you may be *filled to the measure of all the fullness of God.* (Eph. 3:16–19)

To "be filled to the measure of all the fullness of God" means to more and more reflect God's righteousness and holiness. This is why Paul wrote to the Romans, "Do not conform any longer to the pattern of this world, but be transformed by the renewing of your mind" (Rom. 12:2). Here it appears that Paul was using the word *mind* to refer, not just to our *intellect,* but to all aspects of our soul, including our emotions and our will.

Principle 3. We must realize that the degree of change that takes place in our body and soul often depends, not solely on our faith, but on the degree to which our total being has been affected by past sins.

Unfortunately, the changes that God wants to take place in our lives are not automatic. We do not immediately become like

Him. Many of us continue to reap what we've sown after we become Christians.

Paul stated this clearly in his letter to the Galatians: "Do not be deceived: God cannot be mocked. A man reaps what he sows. The one who sows to please his sinful nature, from that nature will reap destruction" (Gal. 6:7–8).

We Must Accept Reality

When sin destroys certain aspects of our lives, there is no way to completely undo what we've already done. Sin that has affected our bodies and our psychological nature will continue at times to haunt us, to be a skeleton in our closet. I've seen people become Christians who have had to live with the results of their sin because it has devastated their body and soul. I'm thinking of one man who was an alcoholic. He drank so much over a period of time that it destroyed certain parts of his brain. Fortunately, he was capable of understanding the gospel and eventually became a Christian. Unfortunately, however, God did not restore those sections of his brain that had been destroyed. He suffered the consequences until the day he died and went home to glory. When Christ comes again, he'll receive a brand-new body. His brain will be perfect.

Other people have destroyed their bodies and souls with drugs and continue to reap the results of their actions, even after they become Christians. Others have become HIV positive. Personally, I have never seen anyone with full-blown AIDS completely healed from this disease. I witnessed a wonderful young man who had contracted the AIDS virus through a blood transfusion deteriorate over a period of years and die. Even though the elders of our church anointed him with oil and prayed for his healing, God chose to take him home to heaven.

Could God have healed this young man while he was on this earth? Definitely. But He chose not to, and we must not question God's divine and sovereign decisions. This does not mean that we should not pray for healing. We must always remember that God still sees us as perfect in Jesus Christ.

Don't Settle for Less Than God's Best

This does not mean we should be satisfied with our present state. In some instances, I have seen God respond to prayer and bring unusual healing to both body and soul. Fortunately, not all sins of the past are devastating. God sets in motion a new law in our inner being that can help us rise above many of the affects of sin. We can renew our minds, which in some instances will actually help to renew our bodies. With the help of the indwelling power and presence of the Holy Spirit, no matter what our situation, we can become more and more like our savior. Of all people, Christians should experience the most healing in both body and soul, simply because we're related to the all-powerful God of the universe. As you attempt to personalize these principles, keep in mind Paul's words to the Ephesians: "Now to him who is able to do immeasurably more than all we ask or imagine, according to his power that is at work within us, to him be glory in the church and in Christ Jesus throughout all generations, for ever and ever! Amen" (Eph. 3:20–21).

Personalizing These Principles

Although it is difficult to explain the immaterial part of human beings in a definitive way, I have found the biblical concepts of body, soul, and spirit to be helpful in personalizing and applying the truths we've looked at in this chapter (1 Thess. 5:23; Heb. 4:12). Functionally, these three concepts seem to correlate in many respects with the *physical, psychological,* and *spiritual* dimensions of our personalities, although I'm still not certain what the spirit is like before and after conversion, except that we know from Scripture we're spiritually dead before and spiritually alive after we are born again. As stated earlier, some believe that only the spirit is dead before we're saved, and this is the dimension that becomes totally new when we're converted. Personally, this seems somewhat difficult to prove biblically. Rather, it seems the new birth affects our total being, giving us

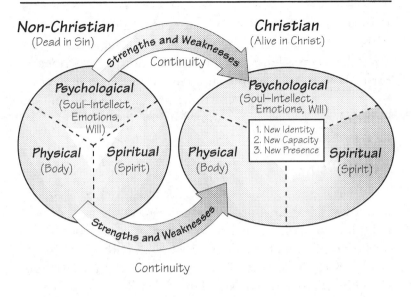

Figure 2

a new identity, a new capacity, and a new presence—the person of the Holy Spirit (see fig. 2).

As you read through the following paragraphs, refer periodically to figure 2. What I'll be sharing with you follows the visual illustration.

The Bible teaches that a person who is not a Christian is spiritually dead (Eph. 2:1). Unbelievers have not been reconciled to God. They do not have eternal life. They do not have a new identity and position in Christ. Nor do they have a new capacity and ability to renew their minds. The Holy Spirit does not dwell in their lives, giving them God's power to live like His Son.

Non-Christians Can Be Very Healthy

Although non-Christians are not alive in Christ, they may function very well physically and psychologically. When Adam and Eve disobeyed God, plunging the whole world into sin, God did not take away our capacity to become balanced personalities in these dimensions of our lives. For example, many of the best athletes in the world are not Christians.

Furthermore, some of the most outstanding intellectual scholars of the world don't even claim to believe in the same God. Some non-Christians I have known are very healthy emotionally, particularly if they have grown up in a secure environment. In fact, many of these people feel quite comfortable without God in their lives. This is one reason why they don't feel a need for Jesus Christ.

The New Birth

What happens, then, when we become believers? First, let's note what doesn't happen. We do not receive a new body (a new physical nature). Neither do we receive a new soul (a new intellect, a new set of emotions, a new will). Rather, we bring to our Christian lives what we are in these areas of our lives, our strengths and our weaknesses. Some identify these as our old "flesh patterns."

We do, however, receive a *new identity* and position in Jesus Christ. We are made alive in Christ (Eph 2:4–5). We also receive a *new capacity* that will enable us to grow and develop spiritually, affecting our total being. We receive a *new presence* in the person of the Holy Spirit who can give us power and strength to become more and more like Jesus Christ. Note that all of these benefits are related to all aspects of our total being.

The Process of Change

Keep in mind, however, that if we have sown to the flesh, we have already reaped corruption in our bodies and our souls. Change may come rather slowly, and in some instances we must accept the fact that we have to live our lives on earth with the consequences of our actions.

Ironically, when some people become Christians, emotional and physical problems get worse before they get better. This can be disillusioning in view of what the Christian life is supposed to be. However, it's understandable when we realize that as new Christians grow in Christ, they develop a new conscience and a new standard for deciding what is right and wrong. When they're tempted to sin and indeed fail God by making wrong choices, it goes without saying that their stress and anxiety level will be higher than before.

We must help new Christians understand this dynamic. We must remind them that while we are in a transition from the old to the new life, God still sees us as perfect in Christ. Our sins have been washed away. Although the results of sin may linger, there's no need to allow these skeletons to frighten us and to put us on a guilt trip.

Set a Goal

As you review the principles in this chapter and the practical suggestions for applying these principles in your own life, isolate an area where you need to give special attention. For example, do you feel guilty about things you shouldn't feel guilty about? Are you still punishing yourself for your past sins, even though Christ has forgiven you?

Remember that once Abraham dealt with the problem that was caused by bad decisions, he "moved his tents and went to live near the great trees of Mamre at Hebron, where he built an altar to the LORD" (Gen. 13:18). God wants you to also worship Him, free from the bondage of the past. Whatever your need, set a goal:

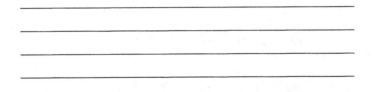

Memorize the Following Scripture

Commit the following Scripture to memory to help you realize your goal:

> *Do not offer the parts of your body to sin, as instruments of wickedness, but rather offer yourselves to God, as those who have been brought from death to life; and offer the parts of your body to him as instruments of righteousness. For sin shall not be your master, because you are not under law, but under grace.*
>
> ROMANS 6:13–14

Growing Together

The following questions are designed for small-group discussion:

1. How has this study helped you understand what happens when we become Christians?

2. What ways have you discovered to keep skeletons from the past from haunting you in the present?

3. Would you feel free to share some of the skeletons you've had to deal with?

4. Do you have a skeleton you are wrestling with at present? If so, would you feel free to share it with us?

5. How can we pray for you specifically?

Chapter 5

A Disastrous Decision
Read Genesis 13:10–12; 19:1–38

One day I began to reflect on men I've known who have made some disastrous decisions. In some instances their marriages disintegrated. Their children were left in a disillusioned state, some denied the faith altogether. Some of these men are still living a double life, claiming to be Christians but living like non-Christians. Some have turned away from God. Some are in prison. Thanks to God's grace, some have made a comeback, but, unfortunately, some are still paying the price for their sins.

A Sad Story

John and Jane (not their real names) attended a Christian college, where they studied the Bible and Christian values. They were both talented musically and ministered together for a number of years. However, at some point in time, they began to question God's authority in their lives. They decided to rear their children in an environment where they gave them total freedom to choose their own faith and lifestyle. They stopped going to church and actually looked down their noses at people who did. They made it clear that they had chosen a "better" way, a more "enlightened" way. John was particularly arrogant about his intellectual capabilities.

I'll never forget the day John called me. Jane had just left him for another man. His children, now teenagers, were both on drugs and living immoral lives. The daughter was in such bad shape she had to be hospitalized.

When I met with John that day, I was talking to a broken-hearted man. He admitted his serious mistake as a husband and father. He confessed his sin and received God's forgiveness, but sadly it was too late to salvage his marriage and his family. The damage had been done. It was a pathetic and sad experience. Although he is now remarried and living in God's will, he looks back on that period in his life as disastrous. To his credit, he has picked up the broken pieces and with God's help has moved forward in the will of God.

Foundations for Disaster

A study of Abraham's life remains incomplete without a careful look at what happened as a result of Lot's selfish and ungrateful decision to leave his uncle and move toward Sodom. That decision was also disastrous. Lot only sank deeper into a life of carnality and deterioration. The tentacles of sin wrapped themselves around his soul and led to a sad and pathetic end. His story demonstrates dramatically what happens when we deliberately disobey and walk outside of God's revealed will.

Why did Lot make such an unfortunate decision to move his tents toward Sodom? What laid the foundations for such a disastrous decision?

What He Saw

Lot "looked up" (Gen. 13:10a). His eyes became windows into his soul which triggered selfish desires that caused him to forget or ignore everything his uncle had ever done for him. Of course, it didn't happen overnight. Lot's disastrous decision did not result from one glance. This kind of decision is always a result of a process. Lot had already had a taste of the good life. Abraham had shared much of his wealth with him. Like most of us, he wanted more. Remember too that he had experienced the lush pasturelands of Egypt, and the Jordan Valley offered the same luxury.

What He Heard

Lot had heard certainly some rather intriguing and spicy stories about the city of Sodom, a place known for its immorality. Our twentieth-century live-sex shows, X-rated movies, and other forms of pornography are mild compared with what was taking place in Sodom. This was Sin City in the Old Testament world, one of the most wicked places anywhere on earth. In fact, as wicked as some of our cities are today, I know of no other city that compares with Sodom's evil practices. The sins of the people who lived there arose like a stench in the nostrils of God.

What He Thought

At some point in time, Lot must have rationalized his decision. Perhaps he thought, *Uncle Abe has more than I have anyway, this will just balance everything out.* Or *Old Uncle Abe is kind of naive, he doesn't really care. After all, he gave me my choice.* Or, regarding Sodom, Lot might have said to himself, *That wicked city really needs a strong witness for the Lord. After all, who's going to tell them about God?* Or perhaps he felt his family needed a broader exposure to the world. After all, his Uncle was getting pretty religious, building altars all over the place and calling on the name of the Lord.

Whatever Lot's rationalizations or excuses, the foundation for his decision was based on his own selfish desires. He didn't consult God about it. In fact, he left God out of the picture completely. He didn't think very long, if at all, about how this decision would affect his uncle. He certainly didn't consider the negative effect the city of Sodom might have upon his children—and himself. His choice was based entirely on what the apostle John calls "the cravings of sinful man, the lust of his eyes and the boasting of what he has and does" (1 John 2:16). What he *saw* and *heard* intrigued him, and without regard for anyone else he rationalized and made this disastrous decision.

Steps That Lead to Disaster

The foundations that led Lot to make this decision cannot be separated from the specific steps he took once he made his decision (Gen. 13:10–12). Read carefully, because these steps are inherent in every decision a man makes, good or bad.

Lot Looked Up and Saw

How many times have you done something wrong or foolish because you allowed your eyes to look at things that are out of harmony with the will of God? Most of our greatest failures can be traced back to the "lust of the eyes." In fact, this is the way sin first entered the human race: "When the woman *saw* that the fruit of the tree was good for food and *pleasing to the eye,* and also desirable for gaining wisdom, she took some and ate it. She also gave some to her husband, who was with her, and he ate it" (3:6).

Many years later one of the most notorious sins in Israel also began with the eyes. One evening, when David had a lot of time on his hands, he "got up from his bed and walked around on the roof of the palace. From the roof he *saw a woman bathing.* The woman was very beautiful, and David sent someone to find out about her" (2 Sam. 11:2–3).

The rest of the story is well known.[1] David sent for Bathsheba and committed adultery. Later, caught in a trap he had set for himself, he committed murder to try to escape the results of his first sin.

David's first sin led to another, one that was even more shameful. As a result, he paid the price for his sins the rest of his life. Although God certainly forgave him because he was truly repentant, David never escaped from the results. It had a devastating impact on his children. Because of their father's poor example, they also committed some horrible sins in Israel.

Lot Chose for Himself

The next step Lot took was to actually make a *choice.* He "chose for himself the whole plain of the Jordan" (Gen. 13:11a). Every sin a man commits is a result of a choice.

Daniel gives us a very positive example in the Old Testament.[2] He stands head and shoulders above many Old Testament saints in demonstrating purity in the midst of temptation. When his eyes were really fascinated with the food and delicacies in the king's palace, even as a young man, he had "resolved not to defile himself with the royal food and wine" (Dan. 1:8). Daniel stuck to his conviction. It affected his choice. By contrast, Lot chose to indulge himself in the cravings of sinful man.

Lot Lived Among the Cities of the Plain

The final step was separation from Abraham. The text reads that they "parted company" (Gen. 13:11), and Lot "pitched his tents near Sodom" (13:12b).

The steps Lot took are very clear. What Lot first *saw* became a lingering *look.* Then he made a *choice,* and finally he *acted* on that choice. He determined to have what he had seen and what he had chosen.

Joseph, however, provides us with another positive example.[3] As a servant in Potiphar's house in Egypt, he was sexually tempted by Potiphar's wife day after day. Yet Joseph had made up his mind that to yield to this temptation would be wrong, a sin against God and his master. One day he was tempted far beyond what he'd seen and heard. Potiphar's wife "caught him by his cloak and said, 'Come to bed with me!'" (39:12).

How easy it would have been for Joseph, like David, to rationalize his behavior. But like Daniel, he had made a decision ahead of time. Consequently, "he left his cloak in her hand and ran out of the house" (39:12).

A Terrible Price to Pay

The steps Lot took led him into very serious trouble (19:1–38). Evidently, the Lord wants us to know exactly how serious that trouble really was since He inspired Moses to record at length all that followed Lot's decision. Although these details are rather graphic—the Bible is an honest book—what happened serves as a serious warning to any man who is tempted to make choices that are similar to Lot's. We cannot play with fire without getting burned.

Lot Was Subject to Terrible Harassment

Any man who makes friends with sinful, wicked people sooner or later will suffer the consequences. This is what happened to Lot. Real friendship is based on mutual respect and concern, not selfishness. Read carefully how Lot's "friends" treated him when he tried to stop them from sexually harassing the two men who were visiting him one evening, in reality, two angels. It's not a pretty picture:

> Before they had gone to bed, all the men from every part of the city of Sodom—both young and old—surrounded the house. They called to Lot, "Where are the men who came to you tonight? Bring them out to us so that we can have sex with them." Lot went outside to meet them and shut the door behind him and said, "No, *my friends.* Don't do this wicked thing." . . . "Get out of our way," they replied. And they said, "This fellow came here as an alien [speaking of Lot], and now he wants to play the judge! We'll treat you worse than them." They kept bringing pressure on Lot and moved forward to break down the door. (Gen. 19:4–7, 9)

Lot Lost the Ability to Make Moral Judgments

It's tragic when a man loses his ability to discern between right and wrong. Lot became inconsistent and confused. His behavior became bizarre. He tried to protect the two men, who were total strangers to him, from sexual abuse and, of all things, offered his own daughters instead (19:8).

I'm almost at loss to try to explain Lot's behavior. I can only conclude that when people fail to obey God in one area of their lives, they often deteriorate in other areas as well. Eventually they lose all sensitivity to sin, particularly in the area of morals.

This is the worst kind of deterioration. This is the kind of environment the apostle Paul was describing in the first chapter of Romans. Sadly, Lot was like an airplane pilot in a thick fog without instruments. He didn't know if he was flying upside-down or right-side up. He lost all sense of spiritual direction. What an incredible warning to everyone in our present cultural climate.

Lot Lost His Influence Over Those Closest to Him

Even the men who were going to marry his daughters lost their respect for Lot. When he tried to warn them of the coming judgment, they ignored him. They didn't even take him seriously. They thought "he was joking" (19:14). They didn't believe in God in the first place, so why should they believe in a coming judgment? They simply kept on eating, drinking, buying, selling, planting, building, and continuing their immoral behavior (Luke 17:28).

Lot Lost the Will to Do What Is Right

This is one of the most serious steps downward in spiritual and moral deterioration. Even though God had revealed His will directly to Lot, he hesitated to leave his sinful environment. When he had warned his sons-in-law of the coming doom and they rejected his overtures, he evidently became so demoralized himself that he lost the will to do what was right.

If it weren't for God's grace and love for Lot and his family, they would have been destroyed with everyone else in Sodom. The Lord had to remove them forcibly from this sinful environment. Listen once again to the Scriptures: "When he hesitated, the men grasped his hand and the hands of his wife and of his two daughters and led them safely out of the city, for the LORD was merciful to them" (Gen. 19:16).

Don't miss an important point in this whole story. Remember that God was showing compassion on Lot only because of Abraham, the man Lot had treated so disgracefully. It was Abraham who had pleaded with God to preserve Lot and his family from total destruction. This once again demonstrates the kind of character Abraham possessed (18:22–33).

Lot Took Advantage of God's Grace

Even in the midst of God's great compassion and all the efforts of others to save him, Lot did not want to obey God completely. The Lord had told him to flee to the mountains to be safe, but he imposed on God's grace and asked for an alternate solution. Once again we see God's compassion. He granted Lot his request to go to a nearby small town, Zoar (19:19–23).

Lot Lost His Most Prized Possession

The most tragic result of Lot's decision to move to Sodom was the lost influence on his wife. She developed such a sense of security with the lifestyle in this sinful place that she could not bear to leave it. Although she was forcibly led out of the city, she wanted to return. Of her own free will, she deliberately disobeyed God and looked back (19:17, 26). Evidently, she also lagged behind, thus when God rained brimstone and fire from heaven Lot's wife became a charred statue. The Scriptures record that "she became a pillar of salt" (19:26).

Imagine the horror that must have gripped Lot. This was the most painful price he had to pay for his decision to expose his family to the wickedness of Sodom.

Lot Committed Incest with His Own Daughters

Because of the sinful influence of Sodom, Lot's daughters also lost their sense of moral rightness. They tricked their father into having sexual relationships with them by getting him drunk. They were more concerned with their own posterity than with obedience to God and respect for their own father (19:30–38). Thus ends a very tragic story. Lot is never mentioned again in the Abrahamic story or in the rest of the Old Testament.

Was Lot a True Believer?

This is a very valid question, especially since the apostle Peter answered this question rather specifically: "If he condemned the cities of Sodom and Gomorrah by burning them to ashes, and made them an example of what is going to happen to the ungodly; and if he rescued Lot, *a righteous man,* who was distressed by the filthy lives of lawless men (for that *righteous man,* living among them day after day, was tormented in his *righteous soul* by the lawless deeds he saw and heard)" (2 Pet. 2:6–8).

Three times Peter used the word *righteous* to describe Lot. This certainly indicates that this man—in spite of his very carnal lifestyle—must have been a true believer. However, he eventually paid a terrible price for his disobedience and unrighteous living. This is one of the ways God disciplines His children when we live in sin. We may not experience immediate judgment from God, but we bring judgment on ourselves through the natural consequences of our sins.

Becoming God's Man Today

Principles to Live By

It's impossible to miss the spiritual principles that emerge from the story of Lot's life. They are crystal clear and specific, and they are reinforced again and again in both the Old and New Testaments.

Principle 1. What we see and hear determines the way we think, and the way we think determines our decisions and actions.

The steps to success or disaster are the same for us today as they were for Lot. Our eyes are the windows to our souls. Our ears become the sound link to hear what is righteous or unrighteous. Together, this dynamic audiovisual human system affects the way we think, and the way we think affects the way we respond to almost all situations. Paul beautifully summarizes this truth in his exhortation to the Philippian Christians:

> Finally, brothers, whatever is true, whatever is noble, whatever is right, whatever is pure, whatever is lovely, whatever is admirable—

if anything is excellent or praiseworthy—*think about such things.* Whatever you have *learned* or *received* or *heard* from me, or *seen in me—put it into practice.* And the God of peace will be with you. (Phil. 4:8–9)

Principle 2. As Christians, we cannot live a carnal life without paying a painful price in our personal lives, in our marriages and family life, and in our relationships with others, both Christians and non-Christians.

Lot is an Old Testament example of a carnal believer. Sadly, his fleshly lifestyle led him to destroy himself. His refusal to do the will of God led to a bitter end. Although eventually he was saved, his whole life was characterized by a miserable existence.

The same thing can happen to each of us. Although the story of Lot is an extreme case, the apostle Paul still warned the Corinthians with language that should grab our attention. Listen to these words:

> For no one can lay any foundation other than the one already laid, which is Jesus Christ. If any man builds on this foundation using gold, silver, costly stones, wood, hay or straw, his work will be shown for what it is, because the Day will bring it to light. It will be revealed with *fire,* and the *fire* will test the quality of each man's work. If what he has built survives, he will receive his reward. If it is *burned up,* he will suffer loss; he himself will be saved, but *only as one escaping through the flames.* (1 Cor. 3:11–15)

Was the apostle Paul thinking about Lot and his experience in Sodom when he penned these final words? If he wasn't, he certainly could have been because it describes this man's life. As we've seen, Lot was probably saved but all of his works were burned up. He literally escaped God's judgment by barely "escaping through the flames." We can only hope that he made positive changes before he was called to his eternal home. If not, he will have no eternal rewards to lay at the feet of Jesus Christ when he stands before God on that final day.

Personalizing These Principles

The story of Lot is an extreme case. Most of us cannot identify directly with the depth to which he fell. But we can certainly identify with the process. Every day of our lives the world holds out its attractions. There are so many things to see, to look at, to think about—things that dull our sensitivity to God and His Word. We don't even have to go looking. These things come to us, right into our homes, particularly by means of television. How easy it is to make choices that are wrong and downright sinful. Before we know it, we find ourselves acting on our choices.

For some of us, it may be an inordinate desire for material things. For others, it may be sexual temptation, particularly through what we see, hear, and think about. For others, it may be a temptation to be prideful and arrogant.

Psalm 1 provides a beautiful pattern for overcoming temptation, making right choices, and experiencing the positive results. As you read this psalm, note the process that is spelled out in verse 1. Once we act on a bad choice, we are seated in the midst of sinful people. This is exactly what happened to Lot. When we encounter him in Genesis 19:1, he is *sitting* in the gate of Sodom.

By contrast, Abraham acted in the direction spelled out in verse 2 of Psalm 1, and the results of his life are graphically illustrated in verse 3. Although Lot appears to have been a true believer, and a carnal one at that, his life on this earth is graphically described in verse 4. The rest of the psalm definitely describes the unrepentant people who lived in Sodom. Read Psalm 1:1–6 and notice the pattern:

1. Blessed is the man who does not *walk* in the counsel of the wicked or *stand* in the way of sinners or *sit* in the seat of mockers.

2. But his delight is in the law of the Lord, and on his law he meditates day and night.

3. He is like a tree planted by streams of water, which yields its fruit in season and whose leaf does not wither. Whatever he does prospers.

4. Not so the wicked! They are like chaff that the wind blows away.

5. Therefore the wicked will not stand in the judgment, nor sinners in the assembly of the righteous.

6. For the LORD watches over the way of the righteous, but the way of the wicked will perish (Ps. 1:1–6).

Set a Goal

Set a goal today that will lead you in the direction of spirituality, not carnality. Be specific. What is your greatest temptation? What is your greatest weakness? Setting a specific goal will program your mind for victory in Jesus Christ, not for failure.

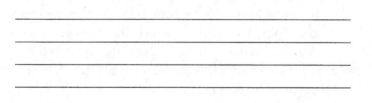

Memorize the Following Scripture

Commit the following Scripture to memory to help you realize your goal:

Finally, brothers, whatever is true, whatever is noble, whatever is right, whatever is pure, whatever is lovely, whatever is admirable— if anything is excellent or praiseworthy—think about such things. Whatever you have learned or received or heard from me, or seen in me—put it into practice. And the God of peace will be with you.
PHILIPPIANS 4:8–9

Growing Together

The following questions are designed for small-group discussion:

1. Why can the average Christian man today identify with Lot's experience?

2. Would you feel free to share with the group an experience in your life that parallels Lot's experience, at least to some degree?

3. How have you learned to "live by the Spirit" and not to "gratify the desires of the sinful nature" (Gal. 5:16)?

4. What can we pray for you specifically?

Chapter 6

A Bout with Fear

Read Genesis 14:1—15:6

*H*ave you ever been traveling along, feeling rather comfortable with your lifestyle? Everything appeared to be going your way. You were decisive, you felt good, your level of self-confidence and energy amazed even you. Most importantly, you felt good about your relationship with God. You were close to Him, and He seemed close to you. You trusted the Lord and you knew you were doing His will—at least most of the time.

Abraham experienced these same spiritual and emotional dynamics after he separated from Lot. Then, like many of us today, particularly when we are making good progress, Abraham faced an emotional and spiritual crisis. His mind and heart suddenly filled with anxiety and fear. He was afraid. What had been dynamic, decisive, and courageous behavior suddenly turned into feeble, ambivalent, and fearful reactions.

What Changed?

What happened to change Abraham's sense of security? To answer this question, we need to reconstruct the events that took place prior to God's revelation to Abraham when He said: "Do not be *afraid*, Abram. I am your shield, your very great reward" (Gen. 15:1).

A Magnanimous Attitude

We've already noted Abraham's unselfish and generous actions toward his nephew, Lot. In the midst of the strife between their herdsmen, Abraham offered Lot an unprecedented choice. He could select the land that best suited him, and Abraham would take what was left.

Lot chose the best, leaving his uncle with the more barren and unproductive areas of Canaan. Abraham's reaction was a remarkable demonstration of self-denial, self-control, and self-sacrifice. In New Testament language, he turned the other cheek toward an ungrateful, self-indulgent, and egotistical relative who was only interested in feathering his own nest.

A Remarkable Defense

When Lot separated from Abraham, he eventually settled in Sodom. It was while he was living there (14:12), that four warring kings swooped down and "seized all the goods of Sodom and Gomorrah and all their food; then they went away. They also carried off Abram's nephew Lot and his possessions, since he was living in Sodom" (14:11–12).

When Abraham heard of Lot's capture, he took action. The Scripture text says it best:

> When Abram heard that his relative had been taken captive, he called out the 318 trained men born in his household and went in pursuit as far as Dan. During the night Abram divided his men to attack them and he routed them, pursuing them as far as Hobah, north of Damascus. He recovered all the goods and brought back his relative Lot and his possessions, together with the women and the other people. (Gen. 14:14–16)

Abraham's move was bold and courageous. He laid his own life and the lives of the men who served him on the line for a selfish and conceited nephew. Here was a gracious and kindhearted man who held no grudges, no bitterness, and no animosity toward a relative who had taken advantage of him. At this moment in his life, Abraham was a marvelous Old Testament example of what it means to do God's will in spite of difficult circumstances and to "do good to them which hate you" and to "pray for them which despitefully use you" (Luke 6:27b, 28b, KJV).

An Outstanding Witness

When Abraham returned from doing battle with the four warring kings, the king of Sodom went out to meet him. He was very grateful for Abraham's kindness. Abraham had recaptured not only Lot, his family and his goods, but he had also set a number of other Sodomites free and had retrieved their possessions. Showing his gratitude, "the king of Sodom said to Abram, 'Give me the people and keep the goods for yourself'" (Gen. 14:21).

Abraham's response must have been shocking to the king: "I have raised my hand to the LORD, God Most High, Creator of heaven and earth, and have taken an oath that I will accept nothing belonging to you, not even a thread or the thong of a sandal, so that you will never be able to say, 'I made Abram rich'" (14:22–23).

Abraham refused to identify with the immorality and degenerate paganism in Sodom. He turned his back on what the world would classify as a golden moment, an opportunity to cash in.

What an example of consistency. Lot had left Abraham with the more unproductive section of Canaan. These selfish actions probably left Abraham to face some really difficult times, a factor that made Abraham's refusal to take the spoils of battle a difficult decision. But he still refused. He let the king of Sodom know—in no uncertain terms, we might add—that he worshiped "the Lord, God Most High" who was capable of meeting all of his physical needs. After all, Abraham believed that his God was the creator of heaven and earth. Since God owns "the cattle on a thousand hills" (Ps. 50:10), Abraham at this moment was able to trust God for his future needs.

From Courage to Fear

What caused Abraham to move from such boldness to a state where it was necessary for God to reassure him with the words, "Do not be afraid, Abram" (Gen. 15:1)? The answer to this question is directly related to what had just happened.

Have you ever made a series of decisions that in retrospect seemed to be naive and reckless? I believe this is what happened to Abraham. When he reflected on what had just transpired, he lost his grip. Think for a moment what he may have been thinking.

Potential Retaliation

Abraham, with his small band of trained men, had taken on four kings with their armies of highly trained warriors. They could have retaliated at any time and wiped out Abraham's household, taken his servants into slavery, confiscated all of his herds, his gold, his silver, and whatever else they might find. It certainly would have been reasonable for Abraham in a moment of reflection to ask himself, *What have I done?* Furthermore, *For what purpose?* The grave answer would have to be, *I've risked my neck and the lives of my whole household for a selfish and ungrateful nephew.*

Potential Poverty

Not only had this Old Testament patriarch risked annihilation and/or slavery, but he had also turned down an offer of material possessions that rightfully belonged to him and that he could certainly have used. Lot had chosen the fertile valley of the Jordan and left Abraham in danger of poverty. His mighty herds and flocks would have quickly eaten every blade of grass that was struggling to grow in this rather desolate land that was just recovering from a very severe famine.

A Human Impossibility

God had promised Abraham a land, a large family that would become a nation, and a special blessing that would affect the whole world. At this point in time, Abraham had no sense of security regarding any of these promises. He must have been doubting everything God had said.

The most pressing problem in Abraham's mind was that he had no natural son. How could he develop into a great nation? At one time he may have thought that Lot might have been the means for God to fulfill His promise. But that hope was quickly dashed when Lot turned away from him and from God.

This was a serious problem for Abraham. This is why he later turned to the Lord, his only source of help, and prayed, "'O Sovereign LORD, what can you give me since I remain childless and the one who will inherit my estate is Eliezer of Damascus?' And Abram said, 'You have given me no children; so a servant in my household will be my heir'" (15:2–3).

God's Reassuring Words

God understood Abraham's plight. He knew he had stepped out in faith and moved into this strange land. He knew that Abraham had unselfishly given up the choicest part of the promised land. He knew that he had rescued an ungrateful nephew. God also knew that he had refused to identify with the world's system.

Furthermore, God understood how Abraham felt regarding the possibility of retaliation from the defeated kings, his fear of poverty from his own actions, and his confusion regarding the impossibility of God's fulfilling His promises without a son.

Given the same set of circumstances, how would you react? Abraham must have gone into shock. But God did not forsake him. He identified with all of his feelings. This is why the Lord reached out to him with a reassuring message. God spoke directly to every one of the events that had brought Abraham into this emotional and spiritual crisis.

I Am Your Shield

Abraham's initial concern was a fear of retaliation. But God promised him He would be his shield against armed warriors.

This is a beautiful Old Testament example of what Paul had in mind when he encouraged the Ephesians to "put on the full armor of God," so that they could take their "stand against the devil's schemes" (Eph. 6:11).

I Am Your Very Great Reward

Abraham's second concern involved his potential poverty. He had just turned down a bountiful reward from the king of Sodom, saying, "I will accept nothing" (Gen. 14:24). Once again, we see God's reassuring words, a restatement of His promise to Abraham that he would be rewarded abundantly for his faithfulness.

So Shall Your Offspring Be

God understood why Abraham was worried and afraid. This is why He once again spoke to Abraham and explained His plan in even greater detail. In the darkness of the night, perhaps when Abraham was tossing and turning on his mat with fear and anxiety, God "took him outside and said, 'Look up at the heavens and count the stars—if indeed you can count them.' Then He said to him, 'So shall your offspring be'" (15:5).

This dramatic and specific word from God once again gave Abraham a sense of security, calmed his nerves, and dissipated his fears. At this point, we are given one of the most significant statements in all of Scripture: "Abram believed the LORD, and he credited it to him as righteousness" (15:6).

What happened in Abraham's heart at that moment? Listen to Paul's explanation as to what transpired that clear, starry night:

> Against all hope, Abraham in hope believed and so became the father of many nations, just as it had been said to him, "So shall your offspring be." Without weakening in his faith, he faced the fact that his body was as good as dead—since he was about a hundred years old—and that Sarah's womb was also dead. Yet he did not waver through unbelief regarding the promise of

God, but was strengthened in his faith and gave glory to God, being fully persuaded that God had power to do what he had promised. This is why "it was credited to him as righteousness." (Rom. 4:18–22)

This was Abraham's moment of personal conversion. Paul went on to explain more specifically what happened that night and how it relates to our own personal salvation:

The words "it was credited to him" were written not for him alone, but also for us, to whom God will credit righteousness— for us who believe in him who raised Jesus our Lord from the dead. He was delivered over to death for our sins and was raised to life for our justification. Therefore, since we have been justi- fied through faith [like Abraham], we have peace with God through our Lord Jesus Christ. (Rom. 4:23–5:1)

No man has ever been saved by works, including Abraham. Salvation has always been by faith. That starry night millenni- ums ago, Abraham simply looked forward to the cross and resurrection, whereas we look back. Naturally, our understand- ing is much greater.

Becoming God's Man Today

Principles to Live By

Few of us today will ever experience what caused Abraham's fear, but we consistently face the same emotional and spiritual dynamics. Although circumstances vary throughout history, our feelings are basically constant. In his basic needs, Abraham was no different than you or I. He was a human being. This is why his experience generates principles that will guide us over the same mountains and through the same valleys.

Principle 1. It's normal to face periods of doubt and fear following great periods of victory in our Christian lives.

There are several reasons why this happens.

Grace for the Moment

First, God often gives us grace to face challenges when they happen, not before. This is certainly what happened to Abraham.

I've seen this happen to many Christians. I'm amazed at how some people are able to endure the crises of life without wavering in their faith. The very week I was preparing this material, I met a woman whose husband is an invalid. He is a stroke victim and unable to care for himself. What makes this particular situation sad is that this man was very active and energetic prior to his illness. He always had a smile on his face and a word of encouragement for everyone. When he greeted me after a church service, he always made me feel like I had delivered the greatest sermon ever preached. He was—and is— a wonderful man of God.

Understandably, this has created a great burden for his wife—physically, emotionally, and spiritually. Yet when she spoke to me, she was praising God for His grace and goodness. "God is so good!" she said. Needless to say, I was blessed and again amazed at God's presence and provision when people face crises that are beyond their control.

Body Chemistry

Second, emotional lows naturally follow emotional highs. Abraham certainly must have experienced this human dynamic. It's related to our body chemistry, not our level of spirituality. Unfortunately, when we're anxious, fearful, and depressed, we tend to put the blame on our relationship with God, wondering if we've failed Him or if He has forsaken us. Not so. Our Father's love and grace never wavers.

The prophet Elijah faced this kind of experience after his great victory on Mount Carmel with the prophets of Baal. When Ahab and Jezebel didn't respond as he had hoped, he wanted to die. The basic reason for this period of depression in his life was that he was physically and mentally exhausted, which contributed to his spiritual disillusionment. Note what God did first. He put him to sleep and provided him with good food (1 Kings 19:1–9).[1]

Steps for overcoming our own periods of doubt and fear are sometimes just as practical. I've seen it work in my own life, and I've seen it work in the lives of others. It's amazing what a good night of rest will do for our perspective, including how we feel about our heavenly Father.

Satanic Attacks

Third, Satan certainly tries to cash in on these periods of physical, emotional, and spiritual exhaustion. This happened to Jesus Christ after He had fasted and prayed in the wilderness for forty days. Satan tempted the Lord to violate His Father's will in the area of pride, power, and possessions (Matt. 4:1–11). If our archenemy attacked Jesus Christ in a moment of weakness, it shouldn't surprise us that he will attack us as well.

Principle 2. Periods of doubt and fear provide opportunities for God to reveal Himself to us in greater measure.

It was during this period of doubt and fear that God revealed Himself to Abraham and reminded him of His presence, His power, and also reassured him that He would never forsake him. The same is true in our lives. As I reflect on my own life, some of my greatest spiritual growth spurts have happened when I felt down and out. It was then that God was able to speak more clearly to me. It was also during these periods that I spoke more consistently with Him.

I have a businessman friend who periodically breaks away from his workaday world and spends a day alone reading the Bible and a good Christian book and spending time in prayer. He reports that the most profitable times are when he is the most stressed out from his work. From a human perspective, it doesn't make sense to break away. There's too much to do. But as a result, my friend regains his physical, emotional, and spiritual equilibrium and renews his strength. He then accomplishes far more in his work in the days that follow. Furthermore, it's during those breakaway moments that he experiences his greatest spiritual growth.

> *Principle 3. During crisis periods in our lives God builds our faith and enables us to believe in Him in ways we've not trusted Him to do before.*

For Abraham this period of doubt and fear resulted in his personal salvation. True, he had been following God's call. The Lord had been leading him and speaking to him. Abraham had even worshiped the Lord with special offerings on the altars he had built in various places in Canaan. But he did not come to understand justification by faith until that night under the stars.

Perhaps this is what God wants to do in your life. You consider yourself a religious man. You go to church regularly. You give your money faithfully to the church. You may have even been baptized. But are you saved? Are you born again? Do you know the Lord Jesus Christ as your personal savior? Have you put your faith in Jesus Christ and in what He has done for you in providing your salvation? If you cannot answer yes to these questions, use this moment to respond to the Holy Spirit's call on your life by receiving the Lord Jesus Christ as your savior.

Personalizing These Principles

To apply these principles to our lives, let's review and illustrate what happened in Abraham's life (see fig. 3). As you follow this visual circle, note that Abraham had a basic need—a need to be reassured and to feel secure. His goal was to do the will of God. His behavior was to step out by faith and obey God. Consequently, he separated from Lot at a loss to himself. Abraham even defended Lot after his nephew turned against him. He also refused to identify with an immoral society.

But in the process, Abraham hit a wall of frustration. He faced the threat of poverty. He faced a strong possibility of

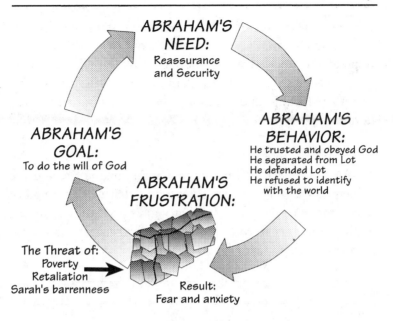

ABRAHAM'S NEED:
Reassurance and Security

ABRAHAM'S BEHAVIOR:
He trusted and obeyed God
He separated from Lot
He defended Lot
He refused to identify
with the world

ABRAHAM'S GOAL:
To do the will of God

ABRAHAM'S FRUSTRATION:

The Threat of:
Poverty
Retaliation
Sarah's barrenness

Result:
Fear and anxiety

Figure 3

retaliation from his enemies. He also faced the fact that he still had no natural heir to fulfill God's promise. The result was fear and anxiety.

Abraham's reaction is a model to us all. It appears he cried out to God. As we've seen, God reassured Abraham that He would help him overcome this wall of frustration.

Can You Identify?

How does all of this apply to you and me? We too face walls of frustration. We have many physical, psychological, and spiritual needs. We will face obstacles in our environment. This naturally creates fear and anxiety. The problem may be financial. We may have a sense of personal inadequacy. We may face social conflicts or we may have physical restraints that keep us from functioning as we would like.

The question all of us must face in applying the principles from Abraham's life is: How am I handling my own frustrations? Remember that fear is a natural reaction. Some Christians—

because of fear—retreat. Others become immobile or unproductive or they may try to run away from the problem. Some respond with anger that gets out of control. In their anger, they become aggressive and try to demolish the wall, caring little about the feelings and needs of others. The results are often devastating.

Set a Goal

As you reflect on this process in Abraham's life and the principles that we've learned, set a goal that will help you to overcome your own fear. If what you've just studied doesn't apply particularly to you, set a goal that will enable you to help someone else handle their fear:

Memorize the Following Scripture

Commit the following Scripture to memory to help you realize your goal:

For God did not give us a spirit of timidity [fear], but a spirit of power, of love and of self-discipline.
                          2 TIMOTHY 1:7

Growing Together

The following questions are designed for small-group discussion:

1. As you've studied this experience in Abraham's life, what have you learned that will help you overcome bouts with fear?

2. Do you remember a time in your life where you experienced a lot of fear after you had experienced a significant victory or successful moment in your life? Would you feel free to share that experience with us?

3. Perhaps you are facing a period of fear right now. Would you feel free to share it with us so that we might pray for you?

4. How have you handled the various walls of frustration that have come into your life?

Chapter 7

A Pure Motive but a Wrong Method
Read Genesis 15:1—16:16

*H*ow many times have you encountered Christians who have right motives, pure hearts, and noble goals, but they spoil everything by using inappropriate methods. In some cases, they may even win a battle and lose the war simply because their strategy for reaching their legitimate goal was a bad choice. There isn't anything so disappointing and painful as to have pure motives and be misinterpreted, misunderstood, criticized, and even rejected and ostracized simply because we've not used good judgment with our methodology.

Don't misunderstand. No matter what our methods, some people will not approve. They simply don't like the goal, as good and right as it may be. Therefore, they'll never approve of your method. We can't please everyone all the time, no matter how hard we try. However, as Jesus taught, we're to be "as wise as serpents and as harmless as doves." Christ's teaching certainly applies to the methods we choose to achieve goals, even Christ-centered ones. It's tragic when our hearts are right and our motives are pure and yet we fail to reach our goals simply because we're insensitive, unwise, too direct, impatient, or we simply do things the wrong way. Abraham dramatically illustrates this predicament. His motives were certainly pure, but unfortunately he made a serious mistake and the results were disastrous.

A Serious Problem

From a human perspective, Abraham faced a serious problem. Ironically, his direct encounter with God, recorded in Genesis 15, added to his dilemma. God spoke to Abraham and confirmed His covenant to make him a father of a great nation. In fact, God became very specific. Abraham's heir would come from his "own body" (15:4). His descendants would be as the stars (15:5). Once again, God reassured Abraham he would take possession of the land (15:7).

This final statement grabbed Abraham's attention since at that moment, the promise of land was uppermost in his mind. Although he was concerned about Sarah's barrenness, he could not help but think about the fact that Lot had just taken possession of the best part of Canaan. Consequently, he addressed this issue with the Lord.

A Valid Question

After God reconfirmed His land covenant verbally, Abraham asked for a sign: "O Sovereign LORD, how can I know that I will gain possession of it?" (15:8). This was a reasonable question, and God responded to Abraham by using a common ceremony, one that was familiar to this Old Testament pilgrim. In those days, two parties would enter into a covenant by selecting certain animals and birds and cutting them in half (except the birds, 15:10). They would lay these animals out in two lines, and then both parties would pass between the lines to confirm the contract. Either party who violated the contract would be subject to the same fate as the animals: death.

A Visible Confirmation

More specifically, God honored Abraham's request by saying, "Bring me a heifer, a goat and a ram, each three years old, along with a dove and a young pigeon" (15:9). Abraham responded immediately by cutting the animals in two and laying them out according to the custom. Then God performed a great miracle: "When the sun had set and darkness had fallen, a smoking firepot with a blazing torch appeared and passed between the pieces. On that day the LORD made a covenant with Abram and said, 'To your descendants I give this land'" (15:17–18a).

Sarah's Barrenness

Even though God visibly affirmed His land promise (15:8), Abraham still faced a perplexing problem. Sarah was still barren. She had never borne children (16:1). To complicate matters, Sarah was already beyond the normal age at which women conceive. How could Abraham and Sarah produce a son? Humanly speaking, it was an impossibility.

Understandably, Abraham was troubled. He had believed God when He had promised him a son, and he still believed God. But as time passed, he became more and more bewildered. It had been more than ten years since he had first entered Canaan. How could God's promise be fulfilled?

A Wrong Method

While Abraham was pondering his plight, Sarah came up with what she thought was a good suggestion. Although it sounds strange—and immoral to us—it made a lot of sense to the culture in which both Abraham and Sarah lived and grew up.

Sarah offered her maid, Hagar, an Egyptian, as a substitute mother. She was probably one of the maidservants Abraham had rescued from Pharaoh. Although unknown to Abraham at this moment, he was about to encounter another problem as a result of his man-centered decision to go to Egypt during the famine (12:10–20).

Sarah used religious reasoning to support her proposal. *"The Lord has kept me from having children,"* she said. "Go, sleep with my maidservant; perhaps I can build a family through her" (16:1–2).

What better rationale could Sarah use than to conclude that God was responsible for their predicament? After all, He had promised Abraham a son who would come from his own body. As far as we know, God had said nothing specifically about Sarah's part in this event. So, reasoned Sarah, since she had never borne children and was now past the age of being able to conceive, could it be that God wanted to use another woman to achieve His purpose?

Four Major Mistakes

Since Abraham was a man who was so intent on doing the will of God, his willingness to father a child by means of a servant girl may shock us. The facts are that Abraham's motive was right. He had absolutely no evil intentions. He wanted to help God achieve His purpose. But even though his motive was right, Abraham's reasoning was faulty. Consequently, he made four major mistakes:

1. A Wrong Premise

Abraham wrongfully assumed that Sarah's reasoning was valid. No doubt about it, she was barren. Furthermore, God hadn't specifically stated that Sarah would be the woman to bear this son. But for Abraham to act on this premise was to limit God, especially in view of the Lord's forthright promise to Abraham.

2. Selfish Motives

On the surface, Sarah's suggestion seemed to be very unselfish. She was concerned about doing God's will. She was also concerned about her husband's emotional state, his perplexity and anxiety resulting from this predicament. God had made him a promise and she wanted to help make it happen. But Sarah's proposal was also prompted by some very selfish motives.

Having mixed motives is not an unusual phenomenon. It's probably impossible for most of us, even as Christians, to always act out of totally pure motives. Underneath we have our own agendas, which are not necessarily selfish or even wrong when these motives involve self-interest. It depends on our ultimate goal. Paul recognized this reality when he exhorted the Philippians to "Do nothing out of *selfish ambition* or vain conceit, but in humility consider others better than yourselves. Each of you should look *not only to your own interests,* but also to the interests of others" (Phil. 2:3–4).

Here Paul recognized that we have our own interests. The point at which we cross the line is when we have a selfish ambition. We are focusing more on ourselves than we are on others. As we'll see, this kind of motivation was inherent in Sarah's proposal. Underneath she had some very selfish motives.

3. Prayerlessness

Somehow it never seemed to enter Abraham's mind to consult the God who had supernaturally led him out of Ur, the One who had preserved his family from annihilation as they had crossed the burning desert, the One who had rescued him from his blunder in Egypt, the One who had just appeared to him in a vision and—with a miraculous sign—confirmed the land promise He had reiterated on several occasions. Somehow it never occurred to Abraham that the One who had denied children to Sarah for so long could just as easily give her a son in her old age. The facts are that Abraham again did not consult God. Where was Abraham's recent perspective on God (Gen. 14:22–23)?

4. Regression

What Sarah had proposed was a very common practice. Archaeologists have discovered tablets containing marriage contracts that "specify that a barren wife must provide a woman for her husband for the purpose of procreation."[1] In fact, we now know that "many of the unusual actions of [both]

Abraham and Jacob with regard to marriage and children can now be understood as being part of the prevailing social culture and laws that Hurrians and Babylonians alike followed for centuries in the Middle East."[2]

At this moment in their lives, both Abraham and Sarah were still in transition. They were still shedding the aspects of their pagan upbringing that were in contradiction to the will of God. Consequently, they both allowed thought patterns and practices they had learned from their pagan culture to influence their thinking.

These cultural dynamics in no way condone Abraham's actions. However, it does help to understand them. Yet while his motive was right, his method was wrong. Although he was sincere in his efforts, he made several serious mistakes. Once again he stepped out of the will of God.

Serious Repercussions

Abraham's mistakes would plague him for years to come. But three things happened immediately:

1. Pride and Arrogance

The moment Hagar conceived, she became proud and arrogant. In fact, she despised Sarah (16:4). Even though he may not have known it in his heart, when Abraham replaced his wife with an Egyptian servant, he violated both God's moral and psychological laws.

God spelled out specifically the results of this kind of sin in Proverbs: "Under three things the earth trembles, under four it cannot bear up: a servant who becomes king, a fool who is full of food, an unloved woman who is married, and *a maidservant who displaces her mistress*" (Prov. 30:21–23).

Hagar's behavior was predictable. If Abraham had stopped to think for a moment before he acted on Sarah's proposal, he might have come to this conclusion on his own. I'm confident he had seen the results of this kind of arrangement before. But more importantly, if he had consulted God, I'm also confident he would have gotten a clear perspective on why this would be a serious error and interfere with God's ideal plan.

2. Bitterness

Predictably, Sarah became bitter and vented her wrath on Hagar. Although only one of the four things listed in Proverbs had taken place, there was a virtual earthquake in Abraham's tent. In her insecurity, Sarah lashed out at Abraham who had simply followed her suggestion. The words are pointed and very painful to Abraham: "Then Sarai said to Abram, 'You are responsible for the wrong I am suffering. I put my servant in your arms, and now that she knows she is pregnant, she despises me. May the LORD judge between you and me'" (Gen. 16:5).

F. B. Meyer captures the irony of Sarah's actions: "How true this is to human nature! We take one false step, unsanctioned by God; and when we begin to discover our mistake, we give way to outbursts of wounded pride. But instead of chiding ourselves, we turn upon others, whom we may have instigated to take the wrong course, and we bitterly reproach them for wrongs in which they, at most, were only instruments, whilst we are the final cause."[3]

3. Family Tension

Not only did Abraham fail to solve the problem of producing a legitimate heir, but he also created an almost unbearable tension in his household. To make matters worse, he would not take responsibility for this action as the head of his household. He dumped the problem back on Sarah. "'Your servant is in your hands,' Abram said. 'Do with her whatever you think best'" (16:6a).

In her state of insecurity and anger, Sarah abused her maidservant. We read that she mistreated Hagar so much so that she fled into the wilderness (16:6b).

Sovereign Intervention

God did not allow Abraham's mistakes to thwart His purpose. He intervened, just as He had done when Abraham erred in Egypt.

An "angel of the LORD found Hagar near a spring in the desert" (16:7a) and told her to return to her home and to submit to Sarah's authority. In the midst of her despair, the Lord also promised her she would have many descendants. Hagar did return, and she bore Abraham a son whom he named Ishmael (16:15).

In spite of Abraham's wrong decision and its unfortunate consequences, God continued to carry out His unconditional promises to Abraham. However, Ishmael's birth began a new chapter in world history that has not yet ended. From Hagar's son has come the great Arab nations who have in recent years been in serious tension with the children of Israel, the promised seed of Abraham. Both groups are still suffering from Abraham's mistakes, mistakes born out of a right motive on Abraham's part but definitely a wrong method.

Coincidentally, in God's scheme of things it's never within His perfect will for a man to have a sexual relationship with any woman other than his wife. Although God tolerated this behavior while He was initially implementing His plan in a sin-sick world, He later made it very clear in the New Testament that a man is to have only one woman in his life—his wife. In fact, Paul specified that this is one of the most significant ways to measure a man's spiritual maturity. He is to be "the husband of but one wife," or more literally, a "man of one woman" (1 Tim. 3:2; Titus 1:6).

Becoming God's Man Today

Principles to Live By

What can we learn from Abraham's mistake that will help us select the right methods for ourselves? First of all, remember that God had not given Abraham specific directions in this matter, only general guidelines, as is often true in our lives today. God has merely given us general principles to guide us in making intelligent decisions.

Don't misunderstand. God's moral instructions are very clear. We know far more than Abraham did at this juncture in his life. It would be many years before God thundered His laws from Mount Sinai and later etched the Ten Commandments on the stone tablets.

However, Abraham's predicament is still relevant today. We can learn from his mistake. There are definite safeguards that we should take in selecting methods to carry out God's will, particularly in matters where the Word of God is basically silent.

Principle 1. In the midst of a crisis, we must be on guard against our human tendency to take matters into our own hands without consulting God and His will for our lives.

When was the last time you said up-front, "What does God want me to do?" Be honest. Isn't the first question we usually ask ourselves when we face a difficult decision, "What can I do?"

To a great extent, this was Abraham's problem. Rather than reflect on previous experiences where he faced similar predicaments, rather than try to learn from past successes and failures, he focused on the existential moment, which always tends to blur our thinking. Unfortunately, Abraham didn't consult God about the matter.

Principle 2. We must be cautious about making quick decisions and snap judgments without thinking through what the end results may be.

This was also part of Abraham's problem. He was not sensitive to God's timing. He got in a hurry. True, ten years seemed like a long time. But a little reflective thinking would have reassured Abraham that God was not in a hurry to work out His plan. The Lord had told him in his previous vision that he would die before the promise of the land to his descendants would be fulfilled. In fact, God also told him his descendants would be in captivity for at least four hundred years before they would settle in Canaan (Gen. 15:12–16). In his frustration, Abraham missed these important clues.

There are times, of course, when we must act quickly. But there are also times when we should wait to take action. It's much better to gain a proper perspective than to rush in and make a serious mistake. Remember too that different problems create an opportunity for God to display His power and guidance. In some situations, this is why He wants us to wait.

Principle 3. We must remember that even those closest to us, those we trust the most, can lead us astray.

Sarah's perspective, although it appeared unselfish, was paganistic, humanistic, and ego-centered. Furthermore, she was very emotionally involved with Abraham. She knew how much he wanted to have a son.

Shouldn't a godly wife (or husband) be able to serve as a good sounding board for decision-making? Yes, but remember that even though Sarah was loyal to Abraham, she was not spiritually mature. Furthermore, even when our wives are godly, sometimes they are so emotionally involved they cannot be objective. In certain situations, it's advisable to consult more objective members of the body of Christ as well as those who are closest to us when we're making important decisions. Be careful not to seek out wisdom from people you think will agree with your perspective, but consult those who will be totally honest and objective.

Please don't misunderstand and use this principle as a rationalization for not listening to your wife. I've discovered over the years that some of the most serious mistakes I've made are when I don't listen to Elaine. A godly woman has a lot of godly wisdom, and we need to listen. The point that we're making here is that in some instances, we need, not only their perspective, but wisdom from other mature believers.

Principle 4. When attempting to determine the will of God, we must be alert to subtle influences from our former lifestyle.

Cultural values have a way of permeating our personalities and molding our thinking. These values often linger in our hearts and minds, even when we become Christians.

This happened to Abraham and Sarah. They made their decision to have Abraham father a child through Hagar because of cultural customs that were operative in their pagan culture. Why not use an approved practice to solve this problem? It seemed logical and rational, particularly since God had promised them a son and Sarah was beyond the age of childbearing.

We must beware then of the custom-made rose-colored glasses we all have as a part of our perceptive apparatus. When we become Christians, we need to check our spiritual and psychological eyesight with the direct teachings of Scripture. Furthermore, we must be careful to interpret Scripture correctly. To do this, consult other mature members of the body of Christ. This process will help us to eliminate the influences of cultural thoughts and ideas that are still embedded in our hearts and minds.

Principle 5. We must always select methods and strategies that are in harmony with the direct teachings and principles of Scripture.

Normally, God does not outline specific methods and strategies for solving problems. Rather, He has given us principles and guidelines for making decisions and specific directives and exhortations. The Ten Commandments are clear-cut. So are the following New Testament exhortations:

> ➤ Therefore each of you must put off falsehood and speak truthfully to his neighbor, for we are all members of one body. (Eph. 4:25)

> ➤ "In your anger do not sin": Do not let the sun go down while you are still angry, and do not give the devil a foothold. (4:26–27)

> ➤ He who has been stealing must steal no longer, but must work, doing something useful with his own hands, that he may have something to share with those in need. (4:28)

➤ Do not let any unwholesome talk come out of your mouths, but only what is helpful for building others up according to their needs, that it may benefit those who listen. (4:29)

➤ And do not grieve the Holy Spirit of God, with whom you were sealed for the day of redemption. (4:30)

➤ Get rid of all bitterness, rage and anger, brawling and slander, along with every form of malice. (4:31)

➤ Be kind and compassionate to one another, forgiving each other, just as in Christ God forgave you. (4:32)

Obviously, these directives are clear. To violate them is to violate the will of God. But there are many situations involving decisions today where God expects us to use our intellects to think our way through these situations and come up with the right decisions. For example, God does not specify in which vocation we should be to make a living. However, He does specify how we are to conduct ourselves in that vocation. Furthermore, He does not dictate which girl we should marry. However, He does specify that we should not be unequally yoked to an unbeliever (2 Cor. 6:14). God does not specify what college or university we should attend. However, He does specify how we should live while we're there.

In making these decisions, we must never select methods that contradict God's nature or the way He works with us. If we do, we'll wind up making the end justify the means, and like Abraham and Sarah, we'll compound our problems. This is why we must always consult *the Word of God* to determine *the will of God.*

Personalizing These Principles

First of all, let's review. As we do, consult figure 4. There was nothing wrong with Abraham's motive or his goal. He wanted to do the will of God and produce a godly seed, as God told

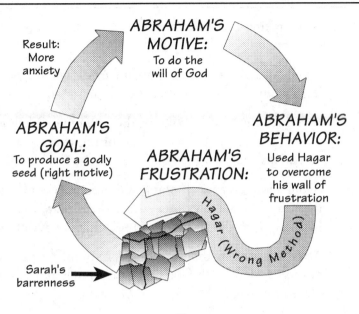

Figure 4

him he should and would. But his wall of frustration was a barren wife.

The result of this frustration was a general state of anxiety. More specifically, he was afraid he would not have an heir as God had promised.

Abraham's method for circumventing his wall of frustration was to follow Sarah's suggestion and father a son through Hagar, her Egyptian maid. Unfortunately, this was a wrong strategy, an inappropriate method, a serious mistake, and it led to increased tension and compounded Abraham's anxiety.

What About You and Me?

Although we may never face the same problems as Abraham, we do face walls of frustration in trying to live life as God intends us to. What may be particularly troublesome is the challenge to make decisions when God does not give specific details to guide us. To avoid making mistakes, always consult the following principles:

1. Avoid taking matters into your own hands without consulting God.

2. Avoid quick decisions and snap judgments without gaining a comprehensive perspective on the situation.

3. Avoid leaning too heavily on the judgments of those closest to you without also consulting other mature Christians.

4. Avoid allowing your thinking and judgments to be influenced by your previous value system that is out of harmony with the teaching and principles of Scripture.

5. Avoid selecting methods to solve your problems that are not in harmony with God's direct teachings and principles in the Word of God.

Set a Goal

As you review these principles, select the one you tend to violate the most in making decisions. For example, you may tend to take matters into your own hands without consulting God. Or you may allow your previous lifestyle and value system to influence you strongly in the decision-making process. Whatever your particular need, set a personal goal:

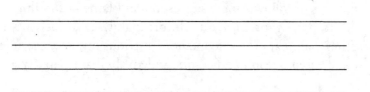

Memorize the Following Scripture

Commit the following Scripture to memory to help you realize your goal:

You, my brothers, were called to be free. But do not use your freedom to indulge the sinful nature; rather, serve one another in love.
GALATIANS 5:13

Growing Together

The following questions are designed for small-group discussion:

1. Why is it easy to select wrong methods and develop inappropriate strategies, even though our motives and goals may be pure and biblical?

2. Would you feel free to share a specific illustration of how this happened in your own life?

3. What resulted and how did you correct the situation?

4. What can we pray for you specifically?

Chapter 8

Thirteen Silent Years

Read Genesis 17:1–27

*I*t's possible for any one of us to make a mistake that can lead to another and then another, even without our knowing it. We can even think we're doing the will of God, that we're on the right path, when in actuality we took a wrong turn sometime back. When this happens, it becomes difficult to admit to ourselves and to others that we've made a mistake. Abraham demonstrates this in a remarkable way.

What is both amazing and startling is that for the next thirteen years of his life, Abraham sincerely believed that he had done the right thing in fathering a child through Hagar. He continued to think he was in the will of God in spite of the family problems created by Ishmael's birth. In fact, Abraham interpreted certain circumstances as a confirmation of God's earlier promise to him when, in fact, these circumstances had nothing to do with God's previous revelation.

Bad Logic

Let's regain perspective. God had promised Abraham a son, an heir. This child would come from Abraham's own body (Gen. 15:4). The Lord, possibly testing Abraham's faith and his reliance on Him for help, did not specifically indicate that

Sarah would be the mother. Since she could not bear children, Abraham reasoned that some other woman should be the mother of his son. So when Sarah suggested that he impregnate her Egyptian slave, Hagar, Abraham willingly participated in the plan. It seemed to be the only logical thing to do.

But Abraham's logic was in error. This was not God's plan. Hagar bore Abraham a son, but he was not the promised seed. Consequently, the moment Ishmael was born, Abraham's family life turned upside-down. Furthermore, the negative results from Abraham's mistaken logic created incredible problems far into the future, even to this day.

Acting on a False Premise

Abraham continued to depend on his faulty logic in evaluating future events. He even concluded that what he saw happening coincided with God's previous promise, which is the most subtle form of confused, self-deceptive thinking.

Let's look again at what happened. Sarah's jealousy exploded in Abraham's face. It then turned into harsh and bitter retaliation against her handmaid, driving Hagar away from home and into the wilderness. When Hagar stopped to rest by a spring, an angel of the Lord appeared and told her to return to Sarah and to submit to her authority (16:9). Then the Lord revealed a very important message to Hagar, one that sounded very familiar to Abraham.

Years earlier, God had reassured Abraham in the midst of his bout with fear with these words: "'Look up at the heavens and count the stars—*if indeed you can count them.*' Then he said to him, 'So shall your offspring be'" (15:5). Now God had appeared to Hagar with a very similar message: "I will so increase your descendants that they will be too numerous to count" (16:10).

It's easy to believe what we want to believe, especially when it's so believable. God's message to Hagar regarding Ishmael led Abraham to another error in logic. Didn't this message from God confirm the fact that Abraham had done the right thing in bringing Ishmael into the world by means of Hagar? After all, Abraham was sincere, and his first decision to produce a son seemed logical in view of God's promise. Furthermore, God's revelation to Hagar regarding Ishmael's future sounded just like His promise to Abraham. Consequently, this Old Testament saint falsely concluded he indeed was within the will of God and that Ishmael was the promised heir.

The Silence of God

Abraham was wrong. Ishmael was not the promised seed. Abraham's false conclusion set the stage for one of the most difficult lessons any child of God can learn. Abraham wandered in the wilderness of his own mistakes for thirteen silent years. He was eighty-six years old when Ishmael was born, and it wasn't until he was ninety-nine that God again appeared to him and spoke directly about His perfect will (16:16; 17:1). Strange as it seems, all during this period of time, Abraham actually believed that Ishmael was the promised seed.

Think of it. In spite of his severe family problems, Abraham struggled ahead, believing he had fulfilled God's promise. How painful this experience must have been. Never, since Abraham left Ur, had God seemed so distant and for such a lengthy period of time.

God was teaching Abraham a dramatic but painful lesson. When we take matters into our own hands and try to do things all by ourselves, God sometimes lets us do it and then allows us to struggle in our own darkness.

But God's purpose is always for our own good, to teach us to trust Him first and foremost rather than putting our confidence primarily on our own abilities. He wants us to consult Him in everything, and all because He wants to direct our paths into His perfect will (Prov. 3:5–6).

This was God's desire for Abraham. Consequently, His loving discipline was at work in this man's life. The next time He spoke to Abraham, God knew He would have a man who would listen very intently, a man whose heart was truly prepared to become the father of many nations.

A Clear Message

When God eventually broke His silence with a direct revelation to Abraham, He made it very clear that the heir He had spoken of more than thirteen years before was not Ishmael (Gen. 17:1–8). The promised son had not yet been born. Sarah was to be the mother, not Hagar nor any other woman (17:16).

What a shock this was to Abraham. For thirteen years, he had believed he was on the right track. Everything had appeared to be so logical, so rational.

A Nervous Laugh

Abraham's response to God's revelation has puzzled many Bible interpreters. We read that "Abraham fell facedown; he laughed" (17:17a).

This does seem like strange behavior since Abraham's mistake was no laughing matter. Why would he question God's power to give Sarah and him a son in their old age, especially in view of God's reassuring words (17:16)? More importantly, why would he cry out to God: "If only Ishmael might live under your blessing!" (17:18)?

Some believe that this must have been an exclamation of joy. But how could it be? I believe this was a nervous laugh. It was a laugh reflecting doubt and confusion—and embarrassment.

Abraham's reactions were those of a man who for thirteen years felt he was right and suddenly discovered he was wrong. He was a man who had placed his total hope in Ishmael as the promised seed. He had come to love this boy in spite of his wild nature (16:12). It was only logical for him to defend himself and his son at this moment, to question God about the event and to plead for Ishmael.

A Clear-cut Answer

God's response to Abraham was both positive and negative. God would bless Ishmael as He had promised (17:20). "But," God said, "my covenant I will establish with Isaac, whom Sarah will bear to you by this time next year" (17:21). It's no wonder

Abraham was shocked, nervous, and nonplused. These promises sounded so similar.

Although Abraham's thought patterns all these years seemed logical and rational, they were built on a false premise that led to false conclusions. Like any one of us, Abraham had difficulty accepting the fact that he had made such a serious mistake. How would you feel if you suddenly discovered that you had been outside of the will of God when for thirteen years you thought you were in the will of God? It would be a shattering blow to any man's ego. Frankly, I'd be on my face laughing, too, not for joy, but from embarrassment.

For the first time in more than a decade, Abraham was able to understand God's revelation to him (15:5) as well as the message God had spoken to Hagar (16:10). Gradually, everything came into focus. God had in mind two sons. The first was Isaac, and the second was Ishmael. The first blessing was for the true heir. The second blessing was for the son who was born according to the flesh. Centuries later, Paul referred to these two boys when he said of Abraham: "His son by the slave woman was born in the ordinary way; but his son by the free woman was born as the result of a promise" (Gal. 4:23).

Back on Track

The most encouraging part of this story is its ending. Abraham, true man of God that he was, took immediate steps to get back on the right track. He acknowledged his error. Although he had to live with the results of his mistake, he immediately began to obey God's Word.

The Lord gave Abraham a new contract, a covenant in the flesh. He and all the males in his family were to be circumcised, which would be a sign of separation from all that is contrary to the will of God. Eager to obey God, Abraham followed through immediately:

> *On that very day* Abraham took his son Ishmael and all those born in his household or bought with his money, every male in his household, and circumcised them, as God told him. Abraham

was ninety-nine years old when he was circumcised, and his son Ishmael was thirteen; Abraham and his son Ishmael were both circumcised on that same day. And every male in Abraham's household, including those born in his household or bought from a foreigner, was circumcised with him. (Gen. 17:23–27)

Becoming God's Man Today

Principles to Live By

How can we avoid Abraham's basic mistake? More specifically, what can we do to make sure we're not a victim of our own subtle self-deception and faulty thinking?

Principle 1. We must beware of Satan's subtle strategy to deceive us.

The father of all liars will do anything he can to lead us astray. He may even "masquerade as an angel of light" (2 Cor. 11:14).

The good news is that we can defeat Satan. We can "be strong in the Lord and in his mighty power." We can "put on the full armor of God" so that we can take our stand against the devil's schemes. We can win the battle, if we follow God's battle plan (Eph. 6:10–18).

Principle 2. We must recognize that our own heart is deceitful (Jer. 17:9).

Like Abraham, we may be very sincere in wanting to do God's will, but we will always have a tendency to rely on our own intellect and other abilities. When we do, we'll make mistakes.

For Abraham, one mistake led to another without his knowing it. Because his heart deceived him, Abraham was not aware of his first mistake; consequently, he didn't recognize the second one. In a sense, he was like a pilot flying blind, not because there were no signals, but rather because he attempted to move ahead on his own steam, ignoring the signals. He failed to turn on his two-way radio and consult God. Sound familiar? When was the last time you did the same thing?

Principle 3. We must be aware of our tendency to think subjectively and with personal bias.

If we want something badly enough, we can interpret almost anything as being a positive sign of God's approval and blessing. In this sense, Abraham's experience is intriguing. He was unable to discern subtle distinctions between right and wrong. His subjective thinking was blurred and distorted, even though it appeared to be clear.

Again, this can happen to any one of us.

➤ It can happen when we don't consult God's Word.

➤ It can happen when we ignore the advice of spiritually mature brothers in Christ.

➤ It can happen when our egos get involved and when we try to take matters into our own hands.

➤ It can happen even in a moment when we sincerely desire to do God's will.

When we make a decision without God's leading, believing we are right, we're in danger of attributing the outcome of future activities to our own "right" decision. Like Abraham, we can misinterpret the Word of God, using it to support our prejudices and biases.

Principle 4. We must be on guard against pride.

Once we have made a mistake, it's very difficult to admit to ourselves and to others that we have been wrong. It's traumatic, threatening, and embarrassing to change our thought patterns, to admit we've made a mistake.

Here we can learn another valuable lesson from Abraham. Although it was a difficult revelation for him to accept, he obeyed God immediately. He got back on the right path the very next day. True, he couldn't undo the past. In fact, his mistake would haunt him for years to come. But he obeyed nonetheless. As we'll see, God blessed him for his faithfulness and obedience.

Personalizing These Principles

Do you realize what privileged men we are to have access to biblical truth? We're in a much better position than Abraham to evaluate God's will since we have the completed revelation of God. Although at times the Lord may appear to be silent, in actuality He is not for He has already revealed all we need to know to live in His perfect will. Although we may lose our focus or perspective, we have His written revelation always, and we also have access to the One who authored the Scriptures. If we are Christians, the Holy Spirit indwells our lives, and it is His desire to guide us and direct us into all truth. Whenever we lack wisdom, we can go directly to the Lord in prayer (James 1:5).

Remember too it is never too late to get back on the right track. In some instances, as with Abraham, we may have to carry the burden of our previous mistakes and sins. However, this is no excuse for not being able to enjoy the present and future blessings of being in God's perfect will.

Set a Goal

As you review the four principles to live by, determine where you are most vulnerable. What is the weakest link in your spiritual chain? If you have difficulty discerning what that weakness is, ask the Lord to reveal it to you. Also, consult another mature brother in Christ. Based on your new insights, set a personal goal:

_____

_____

_____

_____

Memorize the Following Scripture

Commit the following Scripture to memory to help you realize your goal:

For the word of God is living and active. Sharper than any double-edged sword, it penetrates even to dividing soul and spirit, joints and marrow; it judges the thoughts and attitudes of the heart.
HEBREWS 4:12

Growing Together

The following questions are designed for small-group discussion:

1. What lesson have you learned from this particular chapter in Abraham's life that is the most meaningful and helpful?

2. In what way can you identify with Abraham's thirteen-year distortion? Can you illustrate this from your own life? More specifically, in what way has your thinking been faulty because you've built your thoughts and conclusions on a false premise?

3. What happened when you got back on track with the Lord? Would you share both the blessings and your struggles?

4. What can we pray for you specifically?

Chapter 9

Out of the Darkness

Read Genesis 17:1–8; Ephesians 4–6

God had not spoken directly to Abraham for thirteen years, ever since he had taken matters into his own hands to produce a godly seed. Abraham was already eighty-six years old when Hagar bore him Ishmael (Gen. 16:16), and he was ninety-nine years old when the Lord appeared to him again (17:1).

The Silence of Winter

"It must have been a terrible ordeal," states F. B. Meyer, "driving him back on the promise which had been given and searching his heart to ascertain if the cause lay within himself. Such silences have always exercised the hearts of God's saints, leading them to say with the Psalmist: 'Be not silent to me: lest, if thou be silent to me, I become like them that go down into the pit' (Ps. 28:1). And yet they are to the heart what the silence of winter is to the world of nature, in preparing it for the outburst of spring."[1]

Not Even a Whisper

It's difficult to identify with Abraham's thirteen silent years. Stop to think for a moment. You and I have the Bible, the revealed Word of God. We can consult it every day. Not only can we sit and read the complete story of Abraham, but we can see his life in total perspective, from Genesis to Revelation.

We know why God called him out of Ur to the land of Canaan. Not only can we read about the history of Israel in Scripture, the nation that was promised to Abraham, but we can follow the history of God's people up to the present moment. We've seen the land restored in 1948, and we're waiting for the next exciting chapter in their history and ours: the Second Coming of Jesus Christ.

Most importantly, we've experienced the blessing that was promised to Abraham, the coming of the Messiah, the Lord Jesus Christ, the Son of God, the savior of the world. This part of the plan is still unfolding and we have the great privilege of carrying that message of hope around the world, a world that Abraham had no idea existed.

Against the backdrop of our own experience, it's difficult to identify with Abraham's limited perspective. God only spoke to him periodically and briefly. As we have seen, it had been thirteen years since he had heard from God directly.

A Human Flight Plan

During this period of time, Abraham had been flying blind, thinking he was following God's plan for his life. No wonder it was an embarrassing and awkward experience for Abraham to come to grips with the fact that he and Sarah had been following a course they had designed. It was their own flight plan. But God had not abandoned Abraham. Although Abraham and Sarah had definitely taken matters into their own hands thinking they were helping God, God's sovereign plan was still on schedule.

Again it's difficult to blend and understand the human and divine factors reflected in these Old Testament stories. Both are happening concurrently. Abraham and Sarah were definitely out of God's will, but at the same time they were also following a course God had designed in eternity that did not interfere with their ability to make wrong decisions and to be responsible for those decisions.

Mind boggling? Yes. But this is why God is God. His sovereignty and our free will are interrelated concepts that we'll never understand completely until we're transported beyond time. Even then, we will spend eternity marveling at the magnificence of it all.

All Things Work Together for Good

God used Abraham's mistake to prepare both him and Sarah for their next significant step of faith. It's during these periods of winter that most of us learn some of our most significant spiritual lessons. For one thing, God gets our attention. We're ready to listen.

This was true in Abraham's life immediately and later in Sarah's. When God spoke again to Abraham, this was His message and Abraham responded. The silence of winter had turned to springtime again. God's message was loud and clear: "I am *God Almighty;* walk before me, and be blameless" (Gen. 17:1).

El Shaddai

God has identified Himself with many names, but this is the first time He revealed Himself as El Shaddai, meaning God Almighty. Prior to this time, Abraham knew Him as Elohim, the God who makes nature, the One who causes it to be, the God who preserves it. El Shaddai, on the other hand, refers to the God who constrains nature, the One who actually causes nature to do what is against itself.

It's one thing for God to have created the universe and its natural laws—to cause the sun, the moon, and the stars to revolve in their orbits, to establish the laws of gravity and other predictable phenomena. But it is yet another thing for God to cause the sun to stand still and the moon to stop as He did when He answered Joshua's prayer during Israel's battle with the Amorites (Josh. 10:12–13). The Scriptures record that "there has never been a day like it before or since, a day when the LORD listened to a man. Surely the LORD was fighting for Israel!" (10:14).

God created nature, and even though He ordained that natural, unchanging laws govern the universe in an orderly and predictable manner, He can reverse or override these laws and work miracles within the natural order of His creation. He is the omnipotent God, El Shaddai, the One who is not limited in power.

The Laws of Reproduction

Abraham and Sarah had yet to discover and trust God as the One who could and would work miracles, particularly in the area of reproduction. They had already come to know God as a personal God, One who loves mankind and wants to communicate with us. They had experienced God as their shield. They had seen Him superintend their lives, protecting them as they journeyed from Ur to Canaan. He had delivered them from the hand of Pharaoh and protected them from the four warring kings of Canaan.

But Abraham and Sarah were unable to understand God's specific promise that they would have a child in a supernatural way. They could only view this natural process through human eyes. They concluded that they had to help God. From their point of view, they didn't believe God was capable of causing Sarah to conceive a child when she was barren, especially since she was already beyond normal childbearing age. This incorrect perspective regarding God's power and ability led them to make their serious mistake.

But God used their error to teach them—and us—a great lesson. He is God Almighty. He is capable of working miracles. He created natural laws, and He can circumvent them.

When God wants to get His special message to mankind, He has chosen to use His power in this way. Millenniums later, Jesus Christ was supernaturally conceived by the Holy Spirit in Mary's womb, again blending divine and human factors. This is one reason He is identified as the God-man. The infinite God was His father and a finite woman His mother.

To verify that Jesus Christ was the "God-man," His heavenly Father enabled Him to work miracles that turned natural laws upside-down. He changed water to wine, bypassing the natural process of growing and harvesting grapes. He healed people who were ill, reversing or prolonging the natural laws of birth and death. He even raised people from the grave once they had already died. With Lazarus, the body had already begun to decay. Jesus Christ walked on the water, defying the laws of gravity. He instantaneously stopped the winds and rains and quieted the raging waves on the sea of Galilee, again defying natural laws.

When God enabled Abraham and Sarah to conceive a child in their old age, all this was a preview of greater things. Isaac, the child of promise, would be the channel to bring Jesus Christ into the world in a miraculous way to be a blessing to all who would listen to His message.

Name Changes are Significant

When God appeared to Abraham with a new name, El Shaddai, He also gave Abraham and Sarah new names. "No longer," said God, "will you be called Abram [meaning, 'exalted father']; your name will be Abraham [meaning, 'a father of a multitude']" (Gen. 17:5). God then spelled out specifically why He had given His servant this new name: "I will make you very fruitful; I will make nations of you, and kings will come from you" (17:6). God also changed Sarah's name: "As for Sarai your wife, you are no longer to call her Sarai; her name will be Sarah [meaning 'princess']. I will bless her and will surely give you a son by her. I will bless her so that she will be the mother of nations; kings of peoples will come from her" (17:15–16).

These new names would be constant, moment-by-moment reminders of God's promise to Abraham and Sarah and His power to fulfill that promise. To change their names the same time He first appeared to Abraham as El Shaddai was just another expression of God's grace and desire to reach out to all people. His silence had not been punishment and revenge, but loving discipline and training to help Abraham and Sarah walk by faith and to fulfill God's perfect will.

Abraham learned that lesson quickly. Listen to the apostle Paul's reflections on what happened:

> Against all hope, Abraham in hope believed and so became the father of many nations, just as it had been said to him, "So shall your offspring be." Without weakening in his faith, he faced the fact that his body was as good as dead—since he was about a hundred years old—and that Sarah's womb was also dead. Yet he did not waver through unbelief regarding the promise of God, but was strengthened in his faith and gave glory to God, being fully persuaded that God had power to do what he had promised. (Rom. 4:18–21)

Walk Before Me and Be Blameless

When the Lord revealed Himself to Abraham, He zeroed in on a second lesson He had been teaching Abraham during the thirteen silent years. "Walk before me," God said, "and be blameless" (Gen. 17:1).

This divine directive from God correlates with His revelation that He is El Shaddai, the Almighty God. When we have a correct perspective on God (who He is and what He has done and is continually doing for us), it should affect the way we live.

Abraham had failed in his walk with God. Although his motives were right, he had sinned nonetheless. He had failed to consult God. He had become impatient. He had taken matters into his own hands. He had departed from God's perfect will. But now, he was ready to listen, to eagerly do what God wanted him to do. We see a man whose heart was warm and tender toward the God he loved even though he failed along the way.

To walk before God and be blameless literally means to be complete or perfect. God was not suggesting He expected Abraham while on this earth to become sinless or perfect in the absolute sense. If this is what God meant, then we would have to conclude that He wanted Abraham to become like Him in his holiness in every respect, which is an utter impossibility.

Abraham had a long way to go in his spiritual growth to reflect God's righteousness, and he would never achieve this goal until he was transported into God's presence.

Even today, those of us who have God's completed revelation in written form as well as in the person of Jesus Christ are always subject to sin and continue to fall short of God's moral perfection and standard. But it is possible to walk before God in such a way that our lives are continually reflecting the life of Jesus Christ more and more. The more we truly come to know God's love, His power and His grace toward us, the more we will want to become like His Son, Jesus Christ, who revealed the Father to us (John 1:14).

A Fascinating New Testament Parallel

The greatest commentary on these two lessons that God taught Abraham and Sarah is Paul's letter to the Ephesians. Of all the New Testament correspondence, this letter (apart from Paul's letter to the Romans) stands out as the most complete in its biblical teaching and doctrine on why we should live a holy life and what God expects.

In the first three chapters of Ephesians, Paul described the mighty power and sovereign grace of God involved in His plan of redemption. Like Abraham and Sarah, God chose us to respond to His grace. Listen to these incredible and mystifying words:

> For he chose us in him before the creation of the world to be holy and blameless in his sight. In love he predestined us to be adopted as his sons through Jesus Christ, in accordance with his pleasure and will. . . . In him we have redemption through his blood, the forgiveness of sins, in accordance with the riches of God's grace that he lavished on us with all wisdom and understanding. (Eph. 1:4–5, 7–8)

This great redemptive plan that is now in process is the fulfillment of the very promise that God made to Abraham—that through him all nations of the earth would be blessed. That promise clearly referred to the coming of the Lord Jesus Christ to be the savior of the world.

Paul was so caught up with the excitement and thrill of presenting this great redemptive plan that he ended the first section of his Ephesian letter with a glorious doxology: "Now to him who is able to do immeasurably more than all we ask or imagine, according to his power that is at work within us, to him be glory in the church and in Christ Jesus throughout all generations, for ever and ever! Amen" (Eph. 3:20–21).

This is why, Paul was saying, we should walk before God in righteousness and holiness. We should be motivated by His sovereign grace and mercy.

Our Christian Walk

Following his presentation in the first three chapters of Ephesians as to who God is and what He has done, is doing, and will do for us as His children, Paul next described how we are to walk before God (Eph. 4:1, 17; 5:2, 8, 15, NASB).

Five times Paul used a very descriptive metaphor. The Greek word is *peripateo.* Unfortunately, when this New Testament word is translated "live" rather than "walk"—as it is in the NIV—we miss the beautiful imagery that Paul wanted to convey. It was the same idea that God had in mind when He told Abraham to "walk before him and be blameless."

The Hebrew word that God used with Abraham is *hawlak.* It's used in the Old Testament nearly three hundred times, and almost 100 percent of those times it is used as a metaphor. A related metaphor is the word for "path," which is used approximately sixty-five times in the Old Testament. For example, this metaphor is beautifully used in Psalm 119 and is very clearly correlated with the metaphor "to walk." We read: "Your word is a lamp to *my feet* and a light for *my path*" (Ps. 119:105).

God's Pathway

I remember my first fishing expedition in Alaska. Nine of us left our home base early one morning in a seaplane and landed in a small cove. We disembarked and climbed up on the beautiful tundra, encased on all sides by mountains, lakes, and streams. At the top of the hill we found a path that cut its way through the beautiful terrain. With a guide in front and one bringing up the rear, we followed that path to our fishing destination. Each guide carried a pistol to protect us from any wildlife that might be tempted to attack us.

The seaplane took off and headed back to its base. As the plane circled and flew over our heads, the pilot tipped the wings. "How nice," I thought. "He's waving good-bye and wishing us a good day." Right? Wrong. We found out that night when we returned to our base that he was warning us that there was a grizzly bear on the same path about two hundred yards behind us.

Fortunately, we never met up with each other. But I'm glad we were on a path that led us to our destination. I'm also glad we had guides who were leading us and protecting us from danger. In that sense, they were like a lamp to our feet and a light to our path. They showed us clearly how and where to walk.

God has a path He wants us to follow in our Christian walk. It's a pathway of holiness and righteousness. When we follow it, it's good, acceptable, and perfect. When we get off the path, we're setting the stage for a period of trouble and difficulty in our lives. We'll end up trying to direct our own lives, and in most instances we'll make a mess of things.

This was God's message to Abraham, and it's His message to us. Let's see how Paul details this message in his letter to the Ephesians.

Walk Worthy

"*Walk in a manner worthy of the calling with which you have been called*" (*Eph. 4:1, NASB*). Paul began this section of his letter with a general exhortation: "I, therefore, the prisoner of the Lord, entreat you to *walk in a manner worthy of the calling with which you have been called*" (Eph. 4:1, NASB).[2]

This is the same lesson God was teaching Abraham many years before. God had graciously and sovereignly called him out of a pagan environment, out of his lostness and had led him to a new country. He had protected him, provided for him, and promised to never forsake him nor his children yet to come. In fact, His promises were eternal. Now, said God, following Abraham's sin with Hagar, "I am God Almighty; *walk before me and be blameless*" (Gen. 17:1). In other words, God was saying, "Walk worthy, Abraham, of your great calling."

"Walk no longer just as the Gentiles also walk" (Eph. 4:17, NASB). After Paul exhorted the Ephesian Christians to walk in a manner worthy of their great calling in Christ, he became more specific. He spelled out how to walk worthy. Since many of these believers were converted out of the pagan world, he followed through with his metaphor and told them to "walk no longer just as the Gentiles also walk." Paul was concerned that these Christians not regress to their pagan way of living.

Again, this is the same lesson Abraham was learning. He had reverted to a pagan lifestyle and practice when he tried to produce the promised seed through Hagar. The Lord did not want him to live this way any longer.

The Gentiles who lived in Abraham's day were no different from first-century Gentiles. They, too, were "darkened in their understanding, excluded from the life of God." They, too, had hardened their hearts and had "given themselves over to sensuality, for the practice of every kind of impurity with greediness" (Eph. 4:18–19, NASB). The scenario Paul described in the first chapter of Romans had come full circle from Abraham's day to Paul's day. So when God said to Abraham, "Walk before me and be blameless," He was telling Abraham what Paul was telling New Testament Christians.

"Walk in love" (Eph. 5:2, NASB). When Jesus Christ, the promised seed of Abraham, paid for the sins of all humanity, He taught all of us the meaning of true love. This is why John wrote: "This is how we know *what love is:* Jesus Christ laid down his life for us. And we ought to lay down our lives for our brothers" (1 John 3:16).

In some respects, Abraham's love for Lot is a prophetic window through which the people of Canaan could look and catch a glimpse of Christ's love. This old patriarch's attitude and behavior toward his nephew were unparalleled in a pagan world where people thought only of themselves. What Abraham did for Lot, however, is just a beginning point in illustrating Christ's love when we see what this Old Testament saint was willing to do with his son, Isaac. Little did Abraham realize at this point in his life how God would test his love and, at the same time, give him an opportunity to demonstrate the same kind of love God had for us when He sacrificed His only begotten Son on an old rugged cross.

"Walk as children of light" (Eph. 5:8, NASB). To walk in a manner worthy of our great calling in Christ, we must also "walk as children of light." In many respects, this is the positive side of Paul's earlier exhortation to walk no longer as the Gentiles also walk (4:17, NASB). They walked in darkness. As believers, we are to reflect the life of Christ who identified Himself as the light of the world. "Whoever follows me," Jesus said, "will never walk in darkness, but will have the light of life" (John 8:12).

The context surrounding Paul's exhortation to the Ephesians elaborates on what Paul really had in mind:

> But among you there must not be even a hint of sexual immorality, or of any kind of impurity, or of greed, because these are improper for God's holy people. Nor should there be obscenity, foolish talk or coarse joking, which are out of place, but rather thanksgiving. . . . For you were once darkness, but now you are light in the Lord. Live as children of light (for the fruit of the

light consists in all goodness, righteousness and truth) and find out what pleases the Lord. Have nothing to do with the fruitless deeds of darkness, but rather expose them. (Eph. 5:3–4, 8–11)

It's also fascinating to note the context in which Jesus claimed to be the light of the world. The Jews who claimed Abraham as their father were not walking in the light. Thus, Jesus indicted them with these powerful words: "'Abraham is our father,' they answered. 'If you were Abraham's children,' said Jesus, 'then you would do the things Abraham did. As it is, you are determined to kill me, a man who has told you the truth that I heard from God. *Abraham did not do such things*'" (John 8:39–40).

What a tribute to Abraham. Jesus was no doubt referring particularly to the time in Abraham's life following the thirteen years when God was silent. With each new revelation from God this Old Testament saint took another step forward. But more than ever, at this moment in his life, he began to walk before God and be blameless.

Walk Carefully

"*Therefore be careful how you walk*" (Eph. 5:15, NASB). Paul began this section in his letter with the general exhortation to walk worthy. He then filled in the details. As Christians, we're not to walk like we used to, regressing to our pagan ways. Rather, we're to "walk in love," the hallmark of Christian maturity (1 Cor. 13:13). We're also to "walk in the light," particularly demonstrating moral purity. Paul then culminated these thoughts with another generalization. "Therefore," he said, "be careful how you walk" (Eph. 5:15, NASB).

Again, Paul explained what he meant. To be careful how we walk means being wise, not unwise. It means making the most of every opportunity. It means to "understand what the Lord's will is" (Eph. 5:15–17).

As a result of his mistake, Abraham was learning to understand God's will more perfectly. What he thought was a wise decision, and may have been by pagan standards, turned out to be very unwise. As usually happens, unwise decisions that lead us out of the perfect will of God, lead us into periods of darkness and difficulty.

Most importantly, Abraham is a model for all of us in the way he responded to God's discipline for making this foolish decision. Unlike some of us, Abraham did not blame God or others for the mess he created. He was probably tempted to blame Sarah, Hagar, or even Ishmael. Furthermore, he could have become angry toward God for not being more specific in His previous revelations. But he was not. Rather, he accepted responsibility for his actions and did not wallow in self-pity. He had acted unwisely, and he proceeded to correct the problem and to walk worthy.

Becoming God's Man Today

Principles to Live By

God's principles for us today are clear from this study, particularly because of Paul's specific exhortations to the Ephesian Christians. Like Abraham, God wants us to walk before Him and be blameless. Again, this does not mean perfection, but our goal should be to more and more reflect God's righteousness and holiness in all that we do. This is what Jesus had in mind in His Sermon on the Mount when He said, "Be perfect, therefore, as your heavenly Father is perfect" (Matt. 5:48). This is a process we sometimes call progressive sanctification.

Principle 1. As Christians, the way we live should reflect our high calling and position in Jesus Christ.

Think for a moment what it means to be "heirs of God and co-heirs with Christ" (Rom. 8:17). We have an eternal inheritance we didn't deserve. As *Christ*ians, we bear "the name that is above every name"—the name of *Christ* (Phil. 2:9). To bring reproach on the name of Christ is to scorn His love and grace and to embarrass and deeply hurt the One who shed His blood that we might have eternal life.

A Royal Mess

To grasp this truth more fully, think in terms of royalty, the metaphor that Paul and other scriptural writers used to describe our calling in Christ. Reflect on what has happened in England with Prince Charles and Princess Diana. They have both scandalized the throne. They have embarrassed their fellow countrymen (at least they ought to be embarrassed). They've brought reproach on the Church of England, which at least claims to follow the teachings of Jesus Christ. They have embarrassed the queen. They have disillusioned their children. All in all, they've been a disgrace to all that royalty stands for.

We Too Are Royalty

What about our lives as children of the King? Just as every prince is heir to the throne through no merit of his own, so we are co-heirs with Christ through no merit of our own. All that we have received is because of God's grace and mercy. We should never scandalize the One who gave His life to redeem us.

The very day I was writing this material, a friend of mine called and reported on a tragic scandal regarding a well-known evangelical pastor, a man who had influenced people worldwide. Sadly, he was being accused of sexual liaisons with a number of women in his church. Even more tragic, his escapades made hard-copy headlines on national television.

When Paul wrote to the Ephesians—and us—he was appealing to our position and calling in Christ as a basis for walking worthy of that calling, not to embarrass the One who gave everything to purchase our redemption, not to scandalize the name of Jesus Christ, not to disillusion other Christians because we're living inconsistent lives, not to cause those who don't know Christ to laugh and make fun of Christianity because we claim to be Christians and yet do not walk worthy of our great calling.

Principle 2. To live a life that honors the name of Christ, we must "be able to test and approve what God's will is— his good, pleasing and perfect will" (Rom. 12:2).

This is the essence of what Paul was teaching in the last three chapters of his letter to the Ephesians. After specifying how to walk worthy of our calling, he summarized with this exhortation: "Therefore do not be foolish, but *understand what the Lord's will is"* (Eph. 5:17).

This conclusion correlates with Paul's exhortation to the Roman Christians when he wrote in Romans 12:

> *Therefore,* I urge you, brothers, in view of God's mercy, to offer your bodies as living sacrifices, holy and pleasing to God—this is your spiritual act of worship. Do not conform any longer to the pattern of this world, but be transformed by the renewing of your mind. *Then* you will be able to test and approve what God's will is—*his good, pleasing and perfect will.* (Rom. 12:1–2)

Paul outlined God's calling in our lives in Romans 1–11, just as he did in Ephesians 1–3. He then specified how to walk worthy of that calling in Romans 12–16, just as he did in Ephesians 4–6. When all of this truth is condensed into one basic concept, it's simply this: *In view of everything that God has done for us, we should live our lives in accordance with the will of God.* This is what Abraham was learning in his own spiritual walk.

Personalizing These Principles

Following are the three basic directives that Paul gave the Ephesian Christians to help them determine if they were walking worthy of their calling in Christ by understanding and following His will. To what extent are you satisfied with your own Christian walk?

1. I am no longer walking the way many non-Christians walk (Eph. 4:17).
   Dissatisfied 1 2 3 4 5 Satisfied

2. I am walking in love, as Christ loved me (Eph. 5:1, NASB).
Dissatisfied  Satisfied

3. I am walking in the light (Eph. 5:8, NASB).
Dissatisfied ◄ 1 ─── 2 ─── 3 ─── 4 ─── 5 ► Satisfied

Set a Goal

As you review the biblical directives and summary principles in this chapter, what specific goal do you need to set for your life? To determine the area in your Christian experience that needs the most attention, go back and read Paul's letter to the Ephesians, particularly chapters 4–6. Pay particular attention to Paul's words in the context surrounding each of the three basic exhortations outlined in the evaluation scale above. Then write out a specific goal:

_____

_____

_____

_____

Memorize the Following Scripture

Commit the following Scripture to memory to help you realize your goal:

Be very careful, then, how you live—not as unwise but as wise, making the most of every opportunity, because the days are evil. Therefore do not be foolish, but understand what the Lord's will is.
EPHESIANS 5:15–17

Growing Together

The following questions are designed for small-group discussion:

1. Why is it important for Christians to pay particular attention to what it means to walk worthy of their calling in Christ?

2. What lessons has God brought into your life to help you learn to walk in His will?

·3. What does it mean to you personally to "be able to test and approve what God's will is—His good, pleasing and perfect will?"

4. What specific prayer needs do you have?

Chapter 10

Sarah's Most Embarrassing Moment
Read Genesis 18:1–15

*A*t the moment I'm penning these words, there's a great movement among Christian men in America. It's called Promise Keepers. It was begun by Bill McCartney when he was head coach at the University of Colorado, and the movement has spread rapidly. Thousands of men have gathered in huge stadiums on weekends to be inspired and encouraged to become men who make a difference for Jesus Christ.

Most Christian women are elated with this movement. For years, many have been waiting and praying for their husbands to become spiritual leaders in their homes and churches. Unfortunately, not all women are as thrilled. They're confused and even threatened by their husband's new fervor and commitment to do God's will. In turn, some husbands can't seem to understand why their wives aren't as enthused and excited as they are, not realizing that it takes time to convince our mates we're really different. This is particularly true when we've not been the spiritual leaders we should have been in the past.

Abraham's Promise-Keeper Experience

In many respects, Abraham faced this predicament with his wife, Sarah. Although she had stood alongside him all these years, she was confused about what had been happening in their lives. This was particularly true after their thirteen-year mistake.

But now Abraham had his own Promise-Keeper experience. In this instance, God was the promise keeper. He appeared to Abraham when he was ninety-nine years old and told him directly— *"I will confirm my covenant"* (Gen. 17:2). In other words, God reassured Abraham He would fulfill His promise to give Abraham a son, not through a surrogate mother, but through his wife, Sarah.

Second-hand Information

As far as we know, God had never spoken directly to Sarah as He had to Abraham. Yet she had followed her husband, leaving the security of Ur to go, of all things, to a land neither she nor Abraham knew anything about. Although she must have had a lot of fear and anxiety, she left another secure environment in Haran and followed Abraham across the burning desert. When they arrived in Canaan and journeyed down to Egypt, she experienced the humility of being a part of Pharaoh's harem.

All along the way, Sarah had experienced her husband's ups and downs emotionally and spiritually. She knew about the promises God had given him, even though she had to take Abraham's word for it. She even tried to help him out by giving Abraham her maidservant, but the plan backfired. In fact, after Ishmael was born she probably had to take a backseat in Abraham's mind and heart. After all, he was "their" only son, a prized possession for every father living in this culture. In this situation, Ishmael was even more special since both of them believed that he was the child of promise.

And now, after thirteen years, Sarah discovered it was all a mistake. She couldn't help but feel that even the good she tried to do was now being "evil spoken of." She was now ninety years old and Abraham has just told her that he had heard from God again, this time making it very clear that she would conceive in her old age. She was skeptical, perhaps even bitter about her difficult life since coming to Canaan. She desperately wanted to be a part of God's plan, but when she tried, she had failed.

Sarah's Skepticism

The following dialogue is fictional. But in view of what we know from this Old Testament story, it certainly reflects what Sarah must have been thinking and feeling at this moment in her life, particularly after Abraham had tried to convince her that she was going to have a child in her old age. Let's listen in on what may have happened:

SARAH: Nonsense, Abraham! You've had another one of those hallucinations. I really thought you were over those problems. It's been thirteen years since you thought you heard God's voice. I really think your "conversations" with God have been in your imagination all along.

ABRAHAM: I know it's hard to believe, Sarah, but I saw Him. I actually saw God. He appeared to me. And I heard His voice, just as I did thirteen years ago. It was no hallucination.

SARAH: Well, what do you *think* He said this time?

ABRAHAM: We made a mistake, Sarah. A bad mistake. I should never have tried to produce a child by Hagar. God has told me very clearly that you are supposed to be the mother of my son, of the promised seed.

SARAH: Me? Now I know you're crazy, Abraham. You know I can't bear children. I never have been able to. And even thirteen years ago, it would have been impossible.

ABRAHAM: That's where we made our mistake. It's not impossible with God. He is God Almighty. He can make it happen, even right now.

SARAH: (Shaking her head) Abraham, have you lost your senses completely? You've even forgotten how old I am! And look at you!

ABRAHAM: You are ninety years old, Sarah. And I am ninety-nine. I know that! And so does God. In fact, that's been part of His plan all along. Our son is to be a miracle child, a child born in our old age.

SARAH: How do you know that?

ABRAHAM: God told me.

SARAH: God told you! God told you! Abraham, I'm fed up with this whole thing. I tried to help God out. And I tried to help you out. Remember? I gave you Hagar, my own personal slave. And what did I get? When she became pregnant, she made fun of me. She laughed at me. And when I drove her out—with *your* permission—God appeared to her and sent her back with that wild kid of yours. (Pause) You know, Abraham, I'll bet she made that whole story up. God didn't speak to her. She just wanted back in our household. Why, I'd like to—

ABRAHAM: (Speaking in a very comforting but firm fashion) Sarah! Sarah!

SARAH: (Sarah breaks down) I'm sorry, Abraham. I'm so confused. I meant well. But it just didn't turn out right. I guess I'm terribly bitter.

ABRAHAM: (Tenderly holding Sarah, pausing until weeping subsides) I know how you feel. It's been a rough thirteen years for all of us. But God hasn't forsaken us, Sarah. I just misunderstood Him. It's my fault, not yours, that all of this has happened.

SARAH: I want to believe you, Abraham. I want to believe that God really will work a miracle. But, right now, (Pause) I just can't.

Still Unconvinced

One thing is certain from the biblical text. Sarah was still not convinced that she could conceive and bear a child in her old age, which is understandable. She really meant well when she gave Hagar to Abraham. Then, when the whole plan backfired and God actually spoke directly to Hagar, something Sarah had not experienced, she must have felt all kinds of negative emotions: jealousy, anger, and even bitterness. After all, she was human. But, as we'll see, God was not insensitive to Sarah's thoughts and feelings. He was working in her life just as He was working in Abraham's. She was just as important in God's plan as her husband. After all, she was to be the mother of the promised seed.

No Choice But to Wait

What was Abraham to do? He faced another serious dilemma (Gen. 18:1–8). He believed God, but his wife didn't. How could he convince her that his experience was real and that God meant what He said?

There wasn't much Abraham could do but pray and wait. He had to turn the problem completely over to God. He was ninety-nine years old and unable to participate in God's plan without experiencing a miracle himself.

But this was more than a back-against-the-wall experience for Abraham. He had also learned a very important lesson. God means what He says. What He promises, He will deliver. He honors our faith.

Abraham waited with an expectant heart. And God did not disappoint him: "The LORD appeared to Abraham near the great trees of Mamre while he was sitting at the entrance to his tent in the heat of the day" (18:1).

There were actually three men who approached Abraham's tent, but he immediately focused his attention on the one he knew was God. "If I have found favor in your eyes, my lord," he said, "do not pass your servant by" (18:3).[1]

Although running to meet a stranger and bowing low to greet him was not unusual in demonstrating Eastern hospitality, Abraham's expectation and excitement surpassed common courtesy. Had he been crying out to God in prayer, seeking His help in his present dilemma? I believe so. The Lord's sudden appearance didn't seem to catch Abraham off-guard. He responded as if he had been expecting something like this to happen.

Abraham's tactic in getting these three men to stay for a while is really quite human and humorous. Inwardly, the Lord Himself must have been smiling when Abraham invited them to stay for something to eat—more literally, a "piece of bread"—and then hastened to kill the fatted calf (vv. 4–8). Once Abraham obtained a commitment from these men to stay for a little snack, Abraham personally supervised the preparation of a fantastic feast. In our day, what was an invitation for hamburgers turned out, by design, to be a steak dinner with all the trimmings.

The Scriptures speak for themselves:

> So Abraham hurried into the tent to Sarah. "Quick," he said, "get three seahs [probably about twenty quarts] of fine flour and knead it and bake some bread." Then he ran to the herd and selected a choice, tender calf and gave it to a servant, who hurried to prepare it. He then brought some curds and milk and the calf that had been prepared, and set these before them. While they ate, he stood near them under a tree. (Gen. 18:6–8)

Abraham knew he was entertaining El Shaddai. He also knew that the Lord God Almighty was the only One who could solve his family problems and help him and Sarah conceive a child.

Eavesdropping Can Be Embarrassing

Following the meal, the Lord turned His attention to the primary reason He had appeared to Abraham by the Oaks of Mamre. At just the right moment, the three visitors posed a question: "Where is your wife Sarah?" (18:9).

The Lord knew that Sarah was sitting behind a thin curtain of camel's hair inside her tent, intently listening to the conversation. Obviously, for her benefit, the Lord repeated His promise to Abraham in her hearing: "I will surely return to you about this time next year, and *Sarah your wife will have a son*" (18:10).

Imagine Sarah's response when she suddenly heard her name. Although indirect, God's message came through loud and clear. Sarah, of course, didn't have a clue as to who was speaking. Consequently, when she heard these words, she was amused. It was such a ridiculous thought—and funny. As she "laughed to herself," she thought: "After I am worn out and my master is old, will I now have this pleasure?" (18:12)

God's plan was right on schedule. He was not caught off-guard with the thoughts that were going through her mind. He understood the doubt and skepticism that controlled her heart. This is why the Lord surprised her, to cause her to do some very serious thinking. He was igniting a spark of faith. You see, Sarah's thoughts and laugh were internal and inaudible. Furthermore, the curtain of camel's hair hid any negative body language. Imagine Sarah's total surprise when the Lord immediately asked Abraham a question: "Why did Sarah laugh?" (18:13).

The second question the Lord raised in Sarah's hearing must have pierced deeply into her heart and soul. While communicating to Sarah the miracle He would perform, He actually performed a miracle. He interpreted the thoughts and emotions in Sarah's mind and soul. Without a visible or audible clue, He exposed her inner being. God was teaching Sarah the very same lesson He had taught Abraham earlier—that He was El Shaddai, the Almighty God, and that He could do anything, even that which is against nature.

This is the same approach Jesus Christ used with the apostle Thomas. After His resurrection, the Lord had appeared to the other ten disciples. But Thomas was absent and when these men reported that they had seen the Lord, Thomas responded with total unbelief: "Unless I see the nail marks in his hands and put my finger where the nails were, and put my hand into his side, *I will not believe it"* (John 20:25).

Eight days later, the Lord once again appeared to His disciples, and this time Thomas was there. Without any communication, without any report from the other apostles regarding the specific content of Thomas' statement, Jesus immediately walked over to Thomas and said: "Put your finger here; see my hands. Reach out your hand and put it into my side. Stop doubting and believe" (John 20:27).

Thomas too was startled. Who had told the Lord what he had said? No one had seen Jesus for a whole week. At that moment, Thomas knew that Jesus Christ had heard him, even though He was not present. He knew that only God could have this kind of divine knowledge. Immediately, he confessed, "My Lord and my God!" (20:28).

A Greater Miracle

Sarah's experience was just as dramatic—even more so. In her case, there was no audible verbalization, only inner thoughts and feelings. There was no opportunity for anyone to communicate her reactions, even if she had later shared them with Abraham. Yet God's response was immediate—and instantaneous.

When the Lord asked Abraham why Sarah had laughed, and more specifically why she didn't believe that she could have a child when she was old, she understandably responded with fear. God had read her thoughts and verbalized them. In fact, she was so frightened, she lied and said, "I did not laugh" (Gen. 18:15). But once again, the Lord's response was immediate, "Yes, you did laugh."

We're not told how long it took Sarah to overcome her embarrassment, to lower her defenses, to admit her bitterness, and to overcome her fear and unbelief, but we do know that she ultimately responded to the Lord. This is affirmed by the Holy Spirit in the New Testament. She appears in the Old Testament

Hall of Faith along with her husband, Abraham. We read: "By faith even Sarah herself received ability to conceive, even beyond the proper time of life, since she considered Him faithful who had promised" (Heb. 11:11, NASB).[2]

Becoming God's Man Today

Principles to Live By

Principle 1. Husbands and wives are not always at the same place in their spiritual growth and maturity.

Abraham illustrates how easy it is for a husband to get out ahead of his wife, particularly when he has had opportunities for spiritual growth and motivation she has not. Every husband should realize this can happen and why it happens. Oftentimes, the best way for a husband to communicate under these circumstances is to demonstrate these changes in his life in the way he treats his wife, not by attempting to change her with minisermons. At the same time, he should wait on God, praying that the Lord Himself will convince his wife regarding her own need to seek to do His will.

The same is true of a wife who is more advanced spiritually than her husband. Unfortunately, this is often the case. The apostle Peter spoke to this issue directly when he said: "Wives, in the same way be submissive to your husbands so that, if any of them do not believe the word, they may be won over without words by the behavior of their wives, when they see the purity and reverence of your lives" (1 Pet. 3:1–2).

Peter then began the next paragraph with these powerful words to husbands: "Husbands, in the same way be considerate as you live with your wives, and treat them with respect as the weaker partner and as heirs with you of the gracious gift of life, *so that nothing will hinder your prayers*" (1 Pet. 3:7).

Principle 2. God is the same God today as He was in Abraham's day.

God is still omnipotent and omniscient. In His essential nature, He is immutable. He is the same yesterday, today, and forever (Heb. 13:8).

But this does not mean that God always does things the same way. Throughout the Bible—our only inerrant and totally accurate account of God's activities—we see a variation in the manifestation of God's miraculous power. Sometimes He responded to specific prayer, and at other times He acted sovereignly apart from human involvement.

For example, on occasions, God opened the wombs of women who could not bear children. As we've seen, Sarah was one of these women. When all is said and done, this was God's decision. He was not responding to human petition. On the other hand, Hannah was also barren, but she prayed fervently for a son and God responded by giving her Samuel (1 Sam. 1:12–20).

Mary, the mother of Jesus, was a recipient of one of God's greatest miracles. She actually conceived a child without a human father. This too was a sovereign act of God. In fact, the angel Gabriel's words to Mary were almost identical in meaning to God's words to Sarah that day near the Oaks of Mamre. Although He asked Abraham the question—"Is anything too hard for the Lord?"—He was really asking this question of Sarah. The answer, of course, was no. When God spoke to Mary through the angel Gabriel, He put both the question and answer together in one profound and startling statement: "For nothing is impossible with God" (Luke 1:37).

It's important to understand that miraculous events were not normative, even in the Bible. They were exceptions in God's plan. God often performed miracles when He wanted to, in His own sovereign way, and for a specific purpose. But the fact that He doesn't override His natural laws every day, doesn't mean that He cannot. This is true of every miracle that is recorded in the Bible. God could repeat them all at any time, any place, and in the life of any person He chooses.

Principle 3. Supernatural events and prayer are frequently associated in Scripture.

Although God may not choose to work miracles on a consistent basis, there's no question that prayer is to be a normative experience for every believer. Furthermore, prayer is often associated with God's power to change things, even to override natural laws.

This is why James encouraged sick people to "call the elders of the church" for prayer (James 5:14). This is why he also encouraged believers to confess their sins to each other and to pray for each other so that they may be healed. James also teaches us that "the prayer of a righteous man is powerful and effective" (5:16).

No one can deny that prayer and God's supernatural power are definitely connected in this passage of Scripture. But just to make sure we understand that, James drew on an Old Testament illustration that clearly demonstrates that God can override natural law: "Elijah was a man just like us. He prayed earnestly that it would not rain, and it did not rain on the land for three and a half years. Again he prayed, and the heavens gave rain, and the earth produced its crops" (James 5:17–18).

Prayer and God's power are definitely connected. However, when we discuss the power of prayer, it's important that we have God's total perspective. Following are some additional principles to guide us as we engage in this divine activity.

Principle 4. As long as we live on this earth, we will never understand completely the way God works in our lives.

God's will and ways are so far beyond ours that we can only catch a small glimpse of who He is and how He works. Paul expressed it profoundly in his letter to the Romans: "Oh, the depth of the riches of the wisdom and knowledge of God! How unsearchable his judgments, and his paths beyond tracing out! 'Who has known the mind of the Lord? Or who has been his counselor? Who has ever given to God, that God should repay him?' For from him and through him and to him are all things. To him be the glory forever! Amen" (Rom. 11:33–36).

The prophet Isaiah captured the same profound truth in the Old Testament: "'For my thoughts are not your thoughts, neither are your ways my ways,' declares the LORD. 'As the heavens are higher than the earth, so are my ways higher than your ways and my thoughts than your thoughts'" (Isa. 55:8–9).

The point is this: as Christians we must not be confused and disillusioned if there are aspects of God's dealings with us that we cannot understand. On the other hand, the Holy Spirit gives us sufficient insight in the whole of Scripture that we can understand God's ways sufficiently to be able to pray and seek His help in the midst of our own human predicaments. This leads us to another principle.

Principle 5. To unlock God's divine resources, we must always pray according to His will.

The apostle John made this point clear: "This is the confidence we have in approaching God: that if we ask anything according to his will, he hears us" (1 John 5:14). John's statement, of course, leads us to a very practical question: How do we know how to pray according to His will? God can certainly reveal His will directly to anyone of us, but there is only one safe, secure way to approach this issue. We must consult the Scriptures, God's special revelation, to help us discover His plans for each of us.

When God's Will Is Clear

For example, I need not pray, "Lord, if it is your will, heal this marriage." I already know it is His will that a marriage be restored. God has clearly stated without qualifications, "Therefore what God has joined together, let man not separate" (Matt. 19:6). Furthermore, I need not pray, "Lord, if it is your will, help this young man live a pure life." God has made this point very clear again and again throughout Scripture (1 Tim. 5:22).

When God's Will Is Not Clear

On the other hand, I cannot pray, "Lord, heal this person from his failing heart," for nowhere in the Bible am I told that God will heal all physical (or even emotional) diseases. If He did, some people would never die from the afflictions that face all of us as we grow older. However, I *can* always pray confidently: "Lord, *if it is your will,* heal this person." But I must add that I can also pray with confidence: "Lord, give this person grace to be sustained through this experience," whether God actually heals them or not. You see, I know God promises grace to His children in these difficult situations. This is His will.

At times, I've seen God heal people when we've prayed according to His will. Many times, I've seen God give grace to those He has not healed.

Principle 6. God is sovereign and in control of all aspects of the universe, but He honors and respects our free will.

This is a divine mystery. We'll never understand it on this side of eternity. God does not force people to do something they do not want to do, even if it is His will. Consequently, I can pray, "Lord, change that person's bitter attitude," and I need not pray, "if it be your will." I already know that it is His will that no Christian be bitter (Eph. 4:31–32). However, if a person chooses to be bitter, God will not force that person to be loving.

We must remember also that God may choose to answer our prayers by using us to confront that person with his bitterness. In fact, it is God's will that we approach that individual lovingly and directly to make him aware of his specific problem and to attempt to set him free from his sin (Gal. 6:1–2). However, we have no guarantee that the individual will respond. Humanly speaking, God has chosen not to violate our free will, even though He could do so.

God has put the responsibility to do what is right on each of us. True, He lovingly disciplines His children as a means to draw us back into His will (Heb. 12:7–8). However, some Christians do not even respond to God's discipline. They choose to go their own way and ultimately pay the consequences for their sins. In some instances, God even chooses to take them home to heaven (1 Cor. 11:27–32).

Personalizing These Principles

The following list will help you evaluate your perspective on God's power, as well as your view of prayer. Check those that may be interfering with your relationship with God:

- ❑ There is definite sin in my life that may be keeping God from answering my prayers.

- ❑ I do not pray regularly, specifically, and persistently, which may be the reason I experience little of God's power in my life.

- ❑ I have a false view of God in that I try to manipulate Him to do what I want rather than what He wills.

- ❑ I know so little of Scripture that I have difficulty praying in His will.

- ❑ Other _____

Set a Goal

As you review the principles in this chapter as well as work through the checklist above, set a personal goal. For example, there may be a definite sin in your life that may keep God from answering your prayers. Do you realize that as a Christian man and husband, your attitude toward your wife may be that particular sin? Listen carefully to what Peter wrote: "Husbands, in the same way be considerate as you live with your wives, and treat them with respect as the weaker partner and as heirs with you of the gracious gift of life, *so that nothing will hinder your prayers*" (1 Pet. 3:7).

Whatever your particular need, set a specific goal that will help you tap God's supernatural power through prayer:

_____

_____

_____

_____

Memorize the Following Scripture

Commit the following Scripture to memory to help you realize your goal:

> *This is the confidence we have in approaching God: that if we ask anything according to his will, he hears us.*
>
> 1 JOHN 5:14

Growing Together

The following questions are designed for small-group discussion:

1. In what ways have you experienced answers to prayer?

2. What is your greatest need when it comes to understanding prayer?

3. What is your greatest need when it comes to engaging in prayer?

4. Why is prayer and God's power an area that is difficult to understand and explain?

5. What is your specific need for prayer?

Chapter 11

Forgiven—But Facing the Consequences
Genesis 21:1–21

One of the most difficult problems most of us face at some point in our lives involves the results of our past mistakes. Some of these problems can be put behind us once and for all, never to raise their ugly heads. In other instances, we face lingering consequences to one degree or another.

For example, I have a friend who, as a non-Christian, operated his business in unethical ways. He kept two sets of books, one set on paper and the second set in his head. The first set reflected his legal business. The second set reflected the things he sold illegally.

Then he became a born-again Christian. Since he had been reared in a religious environment, he knew what he had done was wrong even while he was doing it. Once he became a true believer in Jesus Christ, he also knew immediately what he had to do. First, he stopped doing business illegally. Second, he knew he needed to do what he could to make things right with those he had cheated.

God honored his repentant heart and enabled him to correct his past mistakes and sins and to start over, seemingly without lingering problems. In fact, this man is involved in full-time ministry today. But early on, while his wife watched him minister to others, she had difficulty respecting him for what he had done. For one thing, their rather lavish lifestyle that had been supported by his illegal business changed dramatically—a constant reminder of her husband's past life. Try as she might, she simply couldn't forget the past. Consequently, my friend temporarily withdrew from the ministry and he and his wife sought counseling, where she too eventually experienced emotional healing in a number of areas in her life.

In terms of emotional dynamics, this is what happened to Abraham and Sarah. They made a serious mistake in using Hagar to produce a son. But then, thirteen years later, they discovered the mistake and got back on track spiritually. Isaac was born and everything seemed wonderful for several years. Then it happened. But that's getting ahead of the story.

An Impossibility Becomes a Reality

The day finally arrived. God kept His promise to Abraham and Sarah. For years they had waited, at times doubting, at times confused, at times attempting to take matters into their own hands. But when the time was right, "the LORD did for Sarah what he had promised" (Gen. 21:1).

God Cannot Lie

God exists as the Almighty God. He is omnipotent, all powerful. But one thing He cannot do. He cannot lie. When God makes a promise, He will never break it. You can count on it. God had made a covenant with Abraham and Sarah and He kept that promise. Thus we read: "Sarah became pregnant and bore a son to Abraham in his old age, *at the very time* God had promised him" (21:2).

Centuries later, Paul wrote to Titus regarding God's promise to unveil His great plan of salvation in Jesus Christ. Note carefully the introduction to his letter:

> Paul, a servant of God and an apostle of Jesus Christ for the faith of God's elect and the knowledge of the truth that leads to godliness—a faith and knowledge resting on *the hope of eternal*

life, which God, who does not lie, promised before the beginning of time, and at his appointed season he brought his word to light through the preaching entrusted to me by the command of God our Savior. (Titus 1:1–3)

God's promise to Abraham and Sarah hundreds of years before embraced the same salvation plan that Paul was writing about. It began with God's initial promise to Abraham when he still lived in Ur, a promise that his seed would be a blessing to all families of the earth (Gen. 12:3). Although Abraham had no clue as to what this promise would eventually mean—as we do—God was referring to the blessing of salvation that would come through Jesus Christ.

When the Time Had Fully Come

This was also what Paul was referring to when he wrote to the Galatians: "But when the time had fully come, God sent His Son, born of a woman" (Gal. 4:4).

The birth of Jesus Christ was an extension of God's promise to Abraham and Sarah, for when the time had fully come for them, Isaac was born. From God's perspective, the promised seed was right on schedule.

You Shall Call His Name Isaac

Abraham immediately named his son Isaac, just as God had commanded (Gen. 17:19). A year earlier when God had informed him that Sarah, not Hagar, would bear the promised seed, Abraham—nonplused and confused—fell facedown and laughed and begged that Ishmael might live under God's blessing (17:17–18). God reassured Abraham that He would indeed bless Ishmael (17:20), but He also made it clear that Ishmael was not the promised seed. "Your wife Sarah will bear you a son," God said, "and *you will call him Isaac*" (17:19).

Interestingly and somewhat ironically, the name *Isaac* means "he laughs." It appears that God was responding to Abraham's laughter by saying, "Your laugh of embarrassment and disbelief will be turned into pure joy when you see your unborn son." Furthermore, every time Abraham called his son by name, he would be reminded of this unique conversation with God.

A Laughing Matter

Imagine the reaction Isaac's birth must have had on all those who heard that a ninety-year-old woman and a ninety-nine-year-old man had produced a son (21:6–7). This incredible news spread rapidly. Abraham's servants were certainly overwhelmed, and so were all the other people who lived in Kadesh and Shur. As far as we know, they had never witnessed anything like this before. They couldn't help but be amazed—and amused. Sarah herself testified to this reality when she proclaimed: "God has brought me laughter, and everyone who hears about this will laugh with me" (21:6).

What a contrast to Sarah's previous response when God told her she would have a son in her old age. Inwardly, she had laughed, expressing unbelief and sarcasm. To her it was an impossibility.

But now Sarah's laugh was one of rejoicing and happiness. This was no longer a dream or a figment of someone's imagination as she held little Isaac in her arms. Sarah now laughed out loud and exclaimed: "Who would have said to Abraham that Sarah would nurse children? Yet I have borne him a son in his old age" (21:7).

A Great Feast

Abraham was also beside himself. Think of it. After all these years, he was also holding in his arms the son God had promised him. Abraham, first of all, had Isaac circumcised on the eighth day—just as God had commanded (17:7–14). When Isaac was weaned—probably around age three—Abraham held a great feast (21:8).

This was a great occasion for Abraham. Imagine his exuberance when he reiterated for all to hear that this was the promised seed, the one through whom God would produce a great nation. This was the son who would make Abraham's name great and the one in whom "all peoples on earth will be blessed" (12:2–3).

Happiness Turned Sour

What was a joyous and happy event quickly led to some very negative feelings and reactions. Ishmael expressed intense jealously and mocked Isaac (21:9). This infuriated Sarah, and she vented her anger on both Hagar and Ishmael (21:10). Predictably, Abraham was caught in the middle and became deeply distressed (21:11). Although Isaac was only three years old, we can only imagine the insecurity he felt. There was no way he would not sense the intense unhappiness, anger, and confusion that permeated the environment. But let's look more carefully at what happened.

Ridicule

Ishmael was probably in his midteens. As an alert teenager, he saw clearly what was happening. Ever since he was old enough to understand, he had been told by his parents that he was the promised seed. But for the last three years, he had been getting another message. He discovered his parents had made a serious mistake. Naturally, he would feel deceived and victimized.

Anger welled up within Ishmael as Isaac became the center of attention. The great feast and the glad speeches in Isaac's honor were the last straws for Ishmael. His growing feelings of bitterness erupted with ridicule and mockery (21:9). We can only conjecture what he did and how he did it, but one thing is certain—Ishmael pushed Sarah too far, and she reacted with intense anger.

Resentment

Ishmael's verbal attack on Isaac also surfaced in Sarah's feelings of bitterness and anger she had harbored toward Hagar and Ishmael for a long time. She quickly reverted to old emotional patterns and reactions, a desire to rid her household of this slave girl and her son (16:6; 21:10).

We must not forget this was a replay for Sarah. When Ishmael was born, it was Hagar who had mocked and despised her. Now, it was Ishmael who was despising and mocking Isaac.

How frequently over the years Sarah must have struggled with her negative feelings toward Hagar. How true this is of so many of us. Once we become bitter, it takes very little to regenerate those feelings again. Even when we feel like we've dealt with them, they seem to lie buried just below the surface, ready to erupt at the slightest provocation.

Remorse

Abraham probably thought that the past was dead and buried, that the results of his mistake were behind him. But at this moment he came face to face with the reality that Sarah had not dealt with her negative feelings. They had only been suppressed and were very much alive. When she came running to Abraham, demanding that he "drive out this maid and her son," we read that "the matter *distressed Abraham greatly* because it concerned his son" (21:11). Reading between the lines, Abraham at this moment was stricken with grief and filled with remorse. Today, we would use the word *depressed*. In his mind, he had to be asking the question, Won't the past ever go away?

Acting Responsibly

In many respects, what happened at this moment was a reflection of what had transpired in this couple's relationship years earlier. When Hagar became pregnant with Ishmael, she despised her mistress (16:4). Predictably, Sarah felt the emotional sting from this personal attack and retaliated. However,

she placed the blame on Abraham, even though producing a child through her maidservant had been her own idea. Unfortunately, Abraham didn't handle this situation well. He evaded his responsibilities as head of the household and quickly placed the responsibility for Hagar's future back in her lap and told her to handle the problem (16:6).

This time, however, Abraham had learned his lesson. Although he was deeply distressed when Sarah told him to get rid of Hagar and Ishmael, he responded maturely. Rather than taking his wife's advice, he waited on the Lord for a solution. Although we're not told how long it was before God responded to Abraham's deep concerns, in time, the Lord appeared to Abraham with a very direct and confirming message: "Do not be so distressed about the boy and your maidservant. Listen to whatever Sarah tells you, because it is through Isaac your offspring will be reckoned" (21:12).

Release from Guilt

The Lord knew that as long as Ishmael lived in Abraham's household, it would be difficult for the old patriarch to focus his thoughts on Isaac as the promised seed (21:14–21). Consequently, the Lord put Abraham at ease regarding Hagar and Ishmael and their future. He did not want Abraham to continue to feel that he had abandoned Sarah's maidservant and his son. He had suffered long enough for his mistake.

Understandably, Abraham still had deep feelings of appreciation for Hagar and a special love for Ishmael. He had weathered some very difficult years with his son, teaching him, training him, and learning to appreciate his wild and determined spirit. Ishmael was like a young and frisky colt who had won the heart of his master. Let's not forget that Abraham had been operating on a false premise for a number of years, believing that Ishmael was the promised seed. Even though he knew differently now, he certainly found it intensely difficult to ask Ishmael and his mother to leave with no place to go.

God empathized with Abraham's agony and distress. Consequently, He reassured His friend that He would take care of Hagar and Ishmael. Following is God's specific promise: "I will make the son of the maidservant into a nation also, because he is your offspring" (21:13).

Just as God kept His promise regarding Isaac, He also kept His promise regarding Ishmael. He delivered the bondmaid and her son from death in the desert. Eventually Ishmael married a girl from his mother's country, the land of Egypt. From this union came a great nation, millions of people who to this day occupy the great Arab countries of the world.

Becoming God's Man Today

Principles to Live By

Abraham's experience following the birth of Isaac teaches us some dynamic lessons. Without doubt, Abraham was living in the perfect will of God. He had produced the promised seed by Sarah. He had named him Isaac as God had told him to. He circumcised his son on the eighth day. In grand fashion, he had prepared a feast and had proclaimed to others that Isaac was the child of the promise.

What more could Abraham have done to demonstrate his desire to do God's will? As far as we can tell from Scripture, he had done everything God wanted him to do. Why then did Abraham have to face the distress and depression caused by Ishmael's ridicule and Sarah's hostility? Why wasn't he able to live happily ever after, rejoicing in the fulfilled promise of God? The answer to these questions gives us very important principles to live by to become God's man today.

Principle 1. Most of us will experience the results of past sins at some point in our lives, either from our own mistakes or because of the impact the sins of others have had in our lives.

Abraham was experiencing the results of his previous mistake. He had definitely violated God's will in having a child by

Hagar, even though he thought he was helping God out. Even though it was Sarah's idea, it created bitterness in her heart and eventually jealousy in Ishmael. There was no way to avoid the aftermath of this problem. In the words of Paul, Abraham was reaping what he had sown (Gal. 6:7). The results of certain sins tend to continue to rise and haunt us. Abraham's mistake was one of them.

Few of us are exempt from suffering as a result of past sins, either those we've committed or that others have committed against us. Sometime, somewhere, and under certain conditions we will face the results of these sins and experience a measure of anxiety and stress. Sometimes these experiences jolt us hard, especially when things are going well and when we believe we've put it all behind us. But suddenly, there it looms before us, creating all kinds of emotional and spiritual ambivalence. When this happens, we need to remember another principle that we can glean from Abraham's life.

Principle 2. No matter what the results of sin in our lives, God wants us to accept reality and face the problem maturely and responsibly.

We've already seen that Abraham set the example. Even though he was horribly upset emotionally, he reacted in a mature fashion. He waited on the Lord until he had a clear perspective on the problem. When he understood what God's will was, he then responded accordingly.

At this point in his life, Abraham was able to remove the cause of the problem and still be in the will of God. The same thing is often true in our own lives. When it is, we must take appropriate steps to correct the situation.

In some circumstances, however, it may not be possible to change things without committing another sin. Two wrongs never make a right. We may have to live with the problem, always attempting to do the will of God in spite of our mistakes. Remember, our primary guideline for differentiating between what is right and what is wrong is the Word of God.

In the Bible we discover what we can change and what we cannot.

All of us have done things or have had things done to us that will inevitably create problems in the present as well as in the future. We'll sometimes face additional crises, even though we are faithfully obeying God and following His will at any given moment in our lives. When problems do arise, we must remember Abraham. We must accept the fact that God forgives the sins of the past. What we are facing is not because we're not forgiven but rather, as a result of the realities of life.

We must then consult God's Word for guidance. Once we understand God's will, we must face the problem head on. We should change what we can and then determine to live with what we cannot.

Principle 3. Many problems we face as Christians, both in the present and in the future, are caused by the effects of sin in the world.

No one who understands what the Bible teaches and at the same time has a clear perspective on what is happening in society can deny that we are living in a world contaminated by sin. Because this is true, those who hate God's ways and His standards will often hate us. For example, many Christians work in professions where cheating and dishonesty run rampant. In these circumstances, if we attempt to abide by the standards of Scripture, we will make other people look bad. When this happens, the natural consequence is rejection. We may even be falsely accused.

I have a brother who, while a college student, worked as an orderly in a hospital. He quickly noticed how often the nurses were neglecting patients and not responding to their calls for help. Consequently, he stepped in to help. It didn't take long, however, for him to discover that the nurses on duty didn't appreciate what he was doing. In actuality, he made them look irresponsible and negligent, primarily because he was responding to needs they were purposely neglecting. As long as he chose to remain in this position, he either had to refrain from getting involved with patients and to live with the knowledge that they were being neglected, or if he continued to help them he had to face the fact that he would soon be fired. In this case, he eliminated the dilemma by finding another job.

A dedicated Christian living in a world that has been contaminated by sin has no guarantee that his life will be one of total peace and inner harmony. In fact, at times when we choose to do God's will, we'll find ourselves in the midst of extreme frustration and stress. On the other hand, a Christian who knows he is doing the will of God in spite of persecution and rejection can rest in the fact that he is pleasing God rather than men.

While faulting those who are not Christians, we must also remember that some believers get themselves into trouble because they are insensitive and unwise in their relationships with unbelievers. Paul had something to say about this when he wrote to the Philippian Christians who were serving non-Christian masters: "Do everything without complaining or arguing, so that you may become blameless and pure, children of God without fault in a crooked and depraved generation, in which you shine like stars in the universe as you hold out the word of life" (Phil. 2:14–16a).

As Christians, we must do all we can to serve our employers well. However, we must never purposely put other people down and make them look bad. In our decisions not to compromise, we should remember the words of Jesus Christ, who said: "I am sending you out like sheep among wolves. Therefore be as shrewd as snakes and as innocent as doves" (Matt. 10:16).

Personalizing These Principles

To help you apply the principles we've learned from Abraham's life, use the following checklist to evaluate your present attitudes and actions.

❑ No matter what has happened in my past life, I have confessed my own sins and accepted God's forgiveness.

❑ If the problems I am facing in life have been caused by others who have sinned against me, with an act of the will, I have forgiven them. I am not allowing bitterness and resentment to control my life.

❑ I have faced the reality of my past sins and how they are affecting my life. I am not living in denial or acting irresponsibly. I am changing what I can change and with God's help, I am living with those things I cannot change.

❑ I realize that living for God in a sinful world will always bring a certain degree of emotional and perhaps even physical discomfort. Consequently, I am striving to make sure that I do not cause problems unnecessarily because of my own unwise behavior. I am doing all I can to live for Jesus Christ, in spite of the problems, even though at times it may lead to personal loss and rejection.

Set a Goal

From this personal evaluation, isolate at least one area in your life where you want to focus more intently on doing God's will. For example, you may be operating out of false guilt. Or you may be trying to change things you cannot change. Whatever your particular need, write out a personal goal:

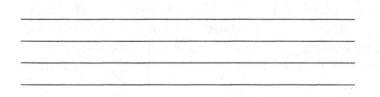

Memorize the Following Scripture

Commit the following Scripture to memory to help you realize your goal:

> *And the Lord's servant must not quarrel; instead, he must be kind to everyone, able to teach, not resentful. Those who oppose him he must gently instruct, in the hope that God will grant them repentance leading them to a knowledge of the truth.*
> 2 TIMOTHY 2:24–25

Growing Together

The following questions are designed for small-group discussion:

1. Would you feel free to share a mistake you've made in your past life that regularly or periodically creates tension and stress in your present relationships?

2. How are you attempting to deal with this problem? Or how have you already dealt with this problem?

3. How have you handled the problem of guilt that often lingers, especially when you cannot resolve the problem completely?

4. Have any of you experienced persecution in your lives simply because you've attempted to do the will of God?

5. What can we pray for you specifically?

Chapter 12

The Final Exam
Read Genesis 22:1–19

I'll never forget my final major examination at New York University before I was awarded my Ph.D. degree. It was an oral test. I'd be anything but truthful if I didn't admit I was anxious and fearful about this forthcoming experience. This was the final step in my educational career, and it would be keenly disappointing and intensely embarrassing to fail.

In reality, I had no justifiable excuse for not passing this exam. I knew it was coming. I had time to prepare. Although I didn't know the particular questions I'd be asked, my faculty adviser briefed me on what to expect. Consequently, I worked hard to be ready. Thankfully, I passed.

When I consider Abraham's final exam, I see some minor similarities to my own, but there are some awesome differences. Like mine, his test was oral in nature, but Abraham's test took place between a man and God Himself.

My test involved a final step in a multiyear process in an academic community, but Abraham faced a challenge to pass a test that culminated a lifetime of experiences in learning to do God's will. To fail my test would have certainly been embarrassing, but it would have only shown up on the screen of human history as an indiscernible blip. If Abraham had failed his test, it would have impacted the course of human history and the eternal destiny of all mankind.

Graduating with Highest Honors

There are other incredible differences between Abraham's test and mine. Although God was preparing His servant for this test, Abraham didn't know it was coming. It was a total surprise. Furthermore, God's final exam was so intense and difficult that no man anywhere on planet Earth has ever faced this kind of experience and probably never will. But in spite of these incredible hurdles, Abraham passed his final exam with highest honors and entered the Hall of Faith. When you browse through this sacred place, you'll find on display a beautiful tribute to this Old Testament great, a tribute that was authored by God Himself. His diploma reads:

> By faith Abraham, when God tested him, offered Isaac as a sacrifice. He who had received the promises was about to sacrifice his one and only son, even though God had said to him, "It is through Isaac that your offspring will be reckoned." Abraham reasoned that God could raise the dead, and figuratively speaking, he did receive Isaac back from death. (Heb. 11:17–19)

The Calm Before the Storm

Following the incredible stress and tension Abraham faced in his family, he entered a period of unprecedented tranquility. He experienced harmony in his family, and he was at peace with his neighbors. More importantly, his relationship with God grew deeper and more meaningful than ever before. He had no greater friend than the One he had come to know and love as the Almighty and Everlasting God (Gen. 17:1; 21:33).

At the human level, Abraham's greatest source of fulfillment focused on his young son, Isaac. As they climbed the gently rolling hills surrounding Beersheba and together viewed the beautiful and productive country to the north, I am confident they often reflected on God's promise to give Abraham and his descendants that land. Isaac's youthful and expectant spirit certainly ignited the old man's heart with incredible joy and excitement. Memories must have often flooded Abraham's soul reminding him of God's faithfulness.

During these days and years of both sunshine and shade under the tamarisk tree he had planted in Beersheba (21:33), little did Abraham realize that this restful and fulfilling experience was preparing him for a severe and sudden storm—an incomparable test of faith. It is a scene in history surpassed only by one other great event: when "God so loved the world that he gave his one and only Son" to die for the sins of the world (John 3:16).

God issued a command to Abraham that confronted him with a choice few men have ever had to make. What the Lord asked Abraham to do must have shattered every nerve in his old and deteriorating body and certainly stretched to the breaking point every bit of spiritual fiber in his faithful soul.

It Didn't Make Sense

What God asked Abraham to do was incongruous. From every human point of view, it was contradictory and inconsistent with the Lord's prior communication. God had promised Abraham that He would establish His covenant with Isaac. It was to be "an everlasting covenant for his descendants after him" (Gen. 17:19). But suddenly and without warning, God spoke to Abraham and said: "Take your son, your only son, Isaac, whom you love, and go to the region of Moriah. Sacrifice him there as a burnt offering on one of the mountains I will tell you about" (22:2).

What made God's command so incongruous is that Isaac was the promised seed, the product of a miraculous conception. All of Abraham's future children were to come from this son. It didn't make sense by any stretch of the imagination for God to ask Abraham to offer Isaac as a sacrifice, to take his life, to literally cut the lifeline that would be the channel through whom God had said He would carry out His promise. There was no earthly way to harmonize God's previous promise with His present command.

Try to put yourself in Abraham's sandals. From his perspective, every detail of God's command was clear. There was no escape route. There were only two alternatives for Abraham: obedience or disobedience. If Abraham chose to obey, it could not be partial obedience. This meant following through on every detail in God's command. It's a choice Abraham made.

An Absolute Step of Faith

While processing this incredible command, we're not told what dialogue Abraham may have had with God (22:3–10). In his humanness, he must have questioned God's directive. The incongruity of it all must have flooded his heart and soul, and the darkness of the night sky must have accentuated the darkness that shrouded his total being. Although Abraham had no doubt witnessed on numerous occasions human sacrifice for sin on Canaanite altars, there was no way he could understand God's command to offer his own son. Abraham had to take an absolute step of faith in the God who had never failed him or let him down.

Thy Will Be Done

Although Abraham's initial reactions to God's command had to have been surprise and shock, when a new day dawned the issue had been settled. We simply read that early the next morning Abraham began to follow through on God's command (22:3). He had experienced God's faithfulness too often to doubt Him now. Although Abraham knew he had to slay his only son—the promised seed—he knew in his heart that God would carry out His promise. The One who cannot lie must have another plan.

For two long days, hand in hand, Abraham and Isaac journeyed toward Moriah. At some point on the third day, they saw the place of sacrifice in the distance. Abraham asked his servants to stay behind while he and Isaac climbed the steep slope together. Isaac's questions must have brought tears to this old man's eyes. He had observed his father sacrifice a lamb to the God of heaven on numerous occasions. But this time there was no lamb. Isaac saw the fire and wood, but he was puzzled. "Where's the lamb for the burnt offering?" he asked his father.

Abraham's response seems to have been quick and reassuring. "God himself will provide the lamb for the burnt offering, my son" (22:8). You see, there was no way Abraham could explain in detail what was happening. He chose to protect Isaac from the fear that must have begun to grip this young boy's heart. Isaac had no doubt also observed Canaanite fathers who had offered their firstborn sons on sacrificial altars to placate the pagan gods. Could it be that his own father was about to offer him as a sacrifice to the God he loved and trusted? But why? His father and his God were friends.

God Could Raise the Dead

Whatever was going through Isaac's mind, Abraham's confident response must have reassured Isaac. Although it's difficult to imagine, Abraham's tone of voice conveyed no sense of insecurity. He knew in his heart that he would once again descend the mountain hand in hand with his beloved son. This is why he told his servants they would *both* come back after they had worshiped God on Mount Moriah (22:5).

Don't misunderstand. Abraham had definitely planned to plunge his knife into his own flesh and blood. But he believed that God would bring Isaac back to life. It was the only way Abraham could reconcile God's previous promise with His present command. This is why the author of Hebrews stated that "Abraham reasoned that God could raise the dead" (Heb. 11:19).

A Voice from Heaven

God honored Abraham's faithful obedience (Gen. 22:11–19). As "he reached out his hand, and took the knife to slay his son," the Lord intervened (22:10). Once again, Abraham heard that familiar voice calling his name, the voice he had heard before. But never had he heard such welcome words: "Do not lay a hand on the boy. . . . Do not do anything to him. Now I know that you fear God, because you have not withheld from me your son, your only son" (22:12).

From God's perspective, Abraham had already offered his son. In his heart, he had made the decision. He was totally willing to take the life of Isaac, believing that God would raise his son from the dead to fulfill His promise (Heb. 11:17–19). In God's eyes, Abraham had passed the course without taking the final exam.

The rest of the story is simply told. The Scriptures speak for themselves:

> Abraham looked up and there in a thicket he saw a ram caught by its horns. He went over and took the ram and sacrificed it as a burnt offering instead of his son. So Abraham called that place The LORD Will Provide. And to this day it is said, "On the mountain of the LORD it will be provided." The angel of the LORD called to Abraham from heaven a second time and said, "I swear by myself, declares the LORD, that because you have done this and have not withheld your son, your only son, I will surely bless you and make your descendants as numerous as the stars in the sky and as the sand on the seashore. Your descendants will take possession of the cities of their enemies, and through your offspring all nations on earth will be blessed, because you have obeyed me." Then Abraham returned to his servants, and they set off together for Beersheba. And Abraham stayed in Beersheba. (Gen. 22:13–19)

The Father of Us All

Abraham left Haran for Canaan at the age of 75 and died at the age of 175 (Gen. 12:4; 25:7). Called out of raw paganism, for more than a century he stands out as one of God's most faithful and obedient Old Testament servants.

Limited Perspectives

We must understand, of course, that his divine perspectives were very limited, but he responded to the light he had. Each time God spoke, he eventually responded, even though he at times wavered, stumbled, and even took matters into his own hands. But even then he was trying to help God. As far as we know, Abraham never deliberately disobeyed God and walked out of His will—as many of us do today. Compared with what Abraham knew about God's will, if each of us responded to what we know today from both the Old and New Testaments, his faith and obedience excels ours in ways that are incomparable. We not only have God's completed revelation in the Holy Scriptures, but we can look back nearly two thousand years and see how God fulfilled His promise to Abraham to bless all nations of the world through Jesus Christ. As Paul wrote to the Galatian Christians: "If you belong to Christ, then you are Abraham's seed, and heirs according to the promise" (Gal. 3:29; also see Rom. 4:16).

From Time to Eternity

What is even more amazing is that Abraham's perspectives on life encompassed more than what he could simply see and feel as he wandered through the land of Canaan. Even though God promised him and his offspring that land, he saw far beyond planet Earth to that heavenly city where all "who are of the faith of Abraham" (Rom. 4:16) will spend eternity. The author of Hebrews captured this reality and provides a wonderful conclusion to his life's story:

> By faith Abraham, when called to go to a place he would later receive as his inheritance, obeyed and went, even though he did not know where he was going. By faith he made his home in the promised land like a stranger in a foreign country; he lived in tents, as did Isaac and Jacob, who were heirs with him of the same promise. *For he was looking forward to the city with foundations, whose architect and builder is God.* (Heb. 11:8–10)

Becoming God's Man Today

Principles to Live By

This dynamic story of Abraham and Isaac on Mount Moriah speaks to people everywhere. There are principles that flow out of this biblical account that apply to all of us, no matter what our ethnic or cultural background and no matter where we live or when. Read carefully. If you allow the Holy Spirit to help you apply these principles, your life could be changed forever.

Principle 1. God does not tempt His children; rather, He tests us.

F. B. Meyer once wrote: "Satan tempts us that he may bring out all the evil that is in our hearts; God tries or tests us that He may bring out all the good."[1] Listen also to James who explains this concept in his New Testament letter:

> Blessed is the man who perseveres under trial, because when he has stood the test, he will receive the crown of life that God has promised to those who love him. When tempted, no one should say, "God is tempting me." For God cannot be tempted by evil, nor does he tempt anyone; but each one is tempted when, by his own evil desire, he is dragged away and enticed. (James 1:12–14)

True, it is often difficult to differentiate between a trial from God and a temptation from Satan. That's because we're limited in our human perspective. The two experiences seem to overlap, and from our limited point of view, they do. But from God's perspective, they're totally separate.

Take Job for example. On the one hand, Satan tried to trip him up, to make him sin, to cause him to turn against God. On the other hand, God was refining Job, strengthening his faith and building his character.

Joseph too experienced this intermingling of temptation and trial. Satan was at work through his brothers. But God was also at work through their evil deeds to accomplish His divine purposes.

Many of us have seen this principle at work in our own lives. I know I have. For example, as I'm writing this chapter, my fellow pastors and support staff at Fellowship Bible Church North are digging our way out of a very severe crisis. An arsonist set a fire in our church office complex that destroyed everything except the contents of our metal file cabinets. All fifteen pastors lost their libraries. As I faced this crisis as the senior pastor, I experienced an unusual challenge: to lead our total staff, lay leadership, and the entire congregation to respond to this crisis in a biblical way.

Ironically, at the very time this crisis hit, I had been teaching Joseph's life's story and had just come to his encounter with his brothers when they had come to Egypt to buy grain. Joseph's perspective on what had happened was magnificent when he told them not to fear any retaliation. "Am I in the place of God?" he asked rhetorically. "You intended to harm me, but God intended it for good" (Gen. 50:19–20).

As I reflected on what had just happened against the backdrop of what I had just been teaching about Joseph's own personal crisis, I was able to view this horrible experience as a test from God, not only for me personally, but also for our total congregation. The arsonist definitely intended to harm us. There is no question about it. It was an act of hatred against us and the gospel of Jesus Christ.

But, you ask, did God intend this for our good? I believe He did. Although we're still viewing this situation through a glass darkly, we're beginning to see more and more clearly the good that is coming out of this crisis. Although I can only begin to reconcile evil and good in the same event, by faith, I know it's possible. It happened to Job, it happened to Joseph, and I believe it happened to us.

Principle 2. *When God tests His children, He prepares us for the trial.*

God never sneaks up on our blind side simply to trip us up, to make us fall. Rather, when God tests us, He wants us to pass, never to fail. Consequently, He prepares us for the crisis.

God did this for Abraham. Prior to his great test, this Old Testament great had experienced unprecedented spiritual growth. His household was in order. He was very secure materially. He had many friends, even among his pagan neighbors. Isaac, the promised son, was his pride and joy. Abraham was very happy in doing the will of God.

There was no doubt in Abraham's mind that God was real. He felt loved and he knew that God considered him His friend. God had prepared him well for this great trial. This is why we read: "Some time later"—after all of these good things had happened—"God tested Abraham" (22:1). When the test came, even though it was very painful, Abraham passed—with an A+.

Here we have a clue as to how we can differentiate temptations from trials. Satan often hits us when we're very weak, when we're not looking. He hits below the belt. He is deceptive and deceitful. He tries to destroy us. This is how he approached Jesus Christ after His forty-day fast in the wilderness (Matt. 4:1–11).

On the other hand, God tests us to build us up. Although He deals with our weaknesses, He prepares us for the trial. Frequently, His tests come after a period of learning about Him, of successes, and even rest and tranquility. This is exactly what happened to Abraham—and Job. Has it ever happened to you?

Principle 3. God's tests may come when we least expect them.

Again we see this in Abraham's experience. Life was flowing very smoothly for this Old Testament saint when suddenly he faced the greatest test of his life. One day everything was great. The next day, Abraham's whole world seemed to be totally threatened.

This is frequently the pattern God follows when He tests Christians. When everything is going smoothly, when we've worked out our problems well at one level, God suddenly tests us to raise us to a whole new level of patience and endurance. This is what James had in mind when he wrote: "Consider it pure joy, my brothers, whenever you face trials of many kinds, because you know that the testing of your faith develops perseverance" (James 1:2–3).

Realize also that Satan often works in a sudden and subtle way, using our moments of strength to also achieve his goals. His plan is never to build character and faith, but to destroy it. Hence, Paul wrote to the Corinthians: "So, if you think you are standing firm, be careful that you don't fall! No *temptation* has seized you except what is common to man. And God is faithful; he will not let you be tempted beyond what you can bear. But when you are tempted, he will also provide a way out so that you can stand up under it" (1 Cor. 10:12–13).

Principle 4. God's tests are often designed to help us grow and mature in our most sensitive and vulnerable areas.

Again, consider Abraham. Abraham loved God. He proved this love by leaving Ur, by wandering in a strange land, by giving up Ishmael. But he also loved Isaac, the child of promise. This young lad had become the center of his life. Perhaps at this moment in his experience, if he were asked whom he loved more—Isaac or God—it may have been difficult for him to answer.

Get the picture? God tested Abraham in the most emotionally sensitive area of his life. Was he willing to put his Lord before Isaac? Was he willing to obey God rather than following his own desires?

You, of course, know what happened. Abraham passed the test. His love for God was stronger than his love for Isaac. He demonstrated this love through unwavering trust and confidence in his heavenly Father.

Today God often tests us in these sensitive areas of our lives. What is most important to us? Where does our security lie? We mustn't be surprised if we're suddenly confronted with a choice between our dearest possessions and the God we also love. It's in moments like these that we begin to understand how deep our love for God really is—or isn't.

Principle 5. God's tests often appear incongruous and illogical.

God's command to Abraham didn't make sense. It appeared inconsistent with what God had already promised him. We can understand why.

The greatest lesson we can learn from a story like this is that as human beings we operate with a limited perspective. What appears illogical to us may be very logical in God's mind. What appears to be a step backward, may ultimately be a step forward. It's at this point, in these moments that seem so irrational and incongruous, we must throw ourselves completely on God. We must trust Him with all our hearts. By faith, we must realize that He cares about us and loves us dearly.

Principle 6. God administers unique tests to special people He has chosen to carry out His purposes in this world.

How true this was in Abraham's life. His trial is a dynamic illustration of God's supreme love for all of us. Never before and never since has God ever asked a man to do what He asked Abraham to do. In fact, God's laws that He later gave to Moses specifically forbade human sacrifice. It is an abomination to Him.

We must remember, however, that Abraham lived long before God ever said anything specific about human sacrifices. In fact, as stated earlier, this Old Testament saint had often witnessed Canaanite fathers offering their firstborn offspring on pagan altars. It was a cardinal principle in their religion, a means of atoning for their sins.

For Abraham his test was related to his cultural background. If pagan deities who were nonexistent demanded such love, was it asking too much for the true God of heaven to require the same? Abraham had no way of perceiving as we do the inconsistency of this request with God's nature. He only knew that God had spoken. Furthermore, he understood the request and he proceeded to obey.

Today, we have God's completed revelation in the Bible and we know that the Lord would never ask any man to offer his son as a human sacrifice. But we also know that what God asked Abraham to do—and then stopped him from doing—illustrates for men and women everywhere the great love God has for all of us.

More specifically, we know from Abraham's experience that the shedding of blood is absolutely essential to atone for sin (Heb. 9:22). But we also know that the blood of bulls and goats and even an innocent lad like Isaac can never satisfy God (Heb. 10:4). There was only one sacrifice that could pay for the sins of the world: the sacrifice of God's one and only Son on Calvary's cross (John 3:16).

At the cross, there was no turning back on God's part. There was no ram caught in the thicket that could suddenly replace the Son of God. The knife had to fall. Without that sacrifice, no man could be saved, not even Abraham and Isaac.

Personalizing These Principles

Spend a few moments thinking about your love for God. How deep is it? Do you worship God because it's the thing to do? Is it simply a token experience of your appreciation for the blessings of life? Or do you love God with your whole heart? Is He truly first in your life?

More specifically, what would be your reaction toward God if He were to ask for your greatest possession, that which means the most to you? How deep would be your love? How strong would be your faith?

Can you pray the following prayer, one you've probably prayed often. But how sincere have you really been when you have mouthed these words?

> Take my life and let it be
> consecrated, Lord, to Thee;
> Take my hands, and let them move
> at the impulse of Thy love.

Take my feet, and let them be
swift and beautiful for Thee;
Take my voice, and let me sing,
always, only, for my King.

Take my lips, and let them be
filled with messages for Thee;
Take my silver and my gold,
not a mite would I withhold.

Take my moments and my days,
let them flow in ceaseless praise;
Take my will and make it Thine,
it shall be no longer mine;

Take my heart, it is Thine own,
it shall be Thy royal throne.
Take my love, my God, I pour
at Thy feet its treasure store;
Take my self, and I will be
ever, only, all for Thee.[2]

Set a Goal

In the light of this study, what goal do you need to set for your life:

_____

_____

_____

_____

Memorize the Following Scripture

Commit the following Scripture to memory to help you realize your goal:

Consider it pure joy, my brothers, whenever you face trials of many kinds, because you know that the testing of your faith develops perseverance.

JAMES 1:2–3

Growing Together

The following questions are designed for small-group discussion:

1. Can you share an experience in your life that illustrates Romans 8:28: "And we know that in all things God works for the good of those who love him, who have been called according to his purpose"?

2. How can we explain crises in our lives that seem totally illogical, that don't make any sense whatsoever?

3. How can we keep from living in fear that the hammer is going to fall when everything seems to be going so well?

4. How can we explain Romans 8:28 to a person who has been terribly wounded by another person? For example, through rape, child abuse, parental neglect, the ravages of war, etc.?

5. What can we pray for you specifically?

Endnotes

Introduction

1. For an in-depth study on the life of Moses, see Gene A. Getz, *Moses: Freeing Yourself to Know God* (Nashville: Broadman & Holman Publishers, 1995).

Chapter 1

1. All emphases in Scripture are added by the author.

2. Abraham's name was originally Abram. God changed his name to Abraham when he was ninety-nine years old (Gen. 17:5). His wife's name was originally Sarai and was changed to Sarah at the same time (17:15; see chapter 9 of this book for a more in-depth explanation on these name changes). For purposes of simplicity and continuity, the names Abraham and Sarah are used throughout this book with the exception of Scriptural quotations where the names Abram and Sarai appear.

3. George Peters, *Biblical Theology of Missions* (Chicago: Moody Press, 1972), 96.

Chapter 2

1. There is a difference of opinion about the place where Abraham received his call. Some believe it was in Haran after he had migrated to the city with his father. But the whole of Scripture

does not seem to affirm this idea. Both the Genesis account (11:31) and the New Testament account (Acts 7:2–4) indicate that Abraham received his call at Ur. The sequence in Genesis 11:31–12:4 becomes very clear if the opening line in Genesis 12:1 is translated, "Now the Lord had said to Abram." This is a permissible translation.

2. F. B. Meyer, *Abraham* (Old Tappan, N.J.: Fleming H. Revell, 1945), 33.

3. Ibid.

4. Personally, I believe divorce is justified if there is persistent sexual unfaithfulness (Matt. 5:31–32) or desertion. In terms of an unsaved mate, Paul stated that "if the unbeliever leaves, let him [her] do so. A believing man or woman is not bound in such circumstances" (1 Cor. 7:15). On the other hand, divorce is a very serious matter and should never be contemplated unless the guidelines of Scripture have been persistently violated.

Chapter 3

1. C. F. Keil and F. Delitzsch, *The Pentateuch* (Grand Rapids, Mich.: Eerdmans Publishing Co.), 197.

Chapter 5

1. For an in-depth study of the life of David, see Gene A. Getz, *David: Seeking God Faithfully* (Nashville: Broadman & Holman Publishers, 1995).

2. For an in-depth study of the life of Daniel, see Gene A. Getz, *Daniel* (Nashville: Broadman & Holman Publishers, 1996).

3. For an in-depth study of the life of Joseph, see Gene A. Getz, *Joseph: Overcoming Obstacles Through Faithfulness* (Nashville: Broadman & Holman Publishers, 1996).

Chapter 6

1. For an in-depth study of the life of Elijah, see Gene A. Getz, *Elijah: Becoming Steadfast Through Uncertainty* (Nashville: Broadman & Holman Publishers, 1995).

Chapter 7

1. *Wycliffe Bible Encyclopedia* (Chicago: Moody Press, 1975), 1:741.

2. Ibid., 1:810.

3. Meyer, *Abraham,* 98.

Chapter 9

1. Meyer, *Abraham,* 102.

2. For an extensive study of this concept, consult Gene A. Getz, *The Walk* (Nashville: Broadman & Holman Publishers, 1994).

Chapter 10

1. The phrase "my Lord" can also be translated "O Lord." In the overall context, it seems that Abraham is addressing one of these men as God Himself.

2. There is a textual variance between the New American Standard and the New International Version. The NASB puts the focus on Sarah's faith; the NIV puts the focus on Abraham's faith. Regarding this variance, New Testament scholar Zane Hodges states: "The NIV interpretation is influenced by the opinion that the phrase *to become a father* (eis katabolen spermatos) can refer only to the male parent, but this need not be so. The writer here chose to introduce his first heroine of faith, one who was able to overlook the physical limitation of her own barrenness to become a fruitful mother." See John F. Walvoord and Roy B. Zuck, *The Bible Knowledge Commentary, New Testament Edition* (Wheaton, Ill.: Victor Books, 1983), 808.

Chapter 12

1. Meyer, *Abraham,* 168.

2. Avis B. Christiansen, 1895.